More Praise for *Young Ar*

"*Young Architects at Play* is as inventive as it is accessible and Filled with compelling and creative ideas and questions, it is a gem of a book and a valuable resource for the classroom and for every educator looking to deepen the learning and play of children."

—**Kelly Blondin,** art specialist, Preschool of the Arts

"A delightful, thorough, must-read primer for teaching architecture to children, Ann Gadzikowski's *Young Architects at Play* reminds us that architecture is personal and intuitive, especially for our youngest learners. Filled with creative, multi-sensory activities, *Young Architects* is an easy-to-read tool for parents and educators alike."

—**Rebecca Boland,** manager of school and family programs, Chicago Architecture Center

"In *Young Architects at Play*, author Ann Gadzikowski explores the interconnectedness of architectural play—play that is inherently complex and interdisciplinary—as children work together to solve challenges ranging from structural engineering and design to artistic and linguistic expression. The book is filled with a depth and breadth of examples, inspiring educators to generate their own classroom examples that challenge the status quo in the field of early childhood education."

—**Alison Maher, MA,** executive director, Boulder Journey School

DISCARD

"*Young Architects at Play* is an insightful tool that can help us build long-overdue connections between the topics of architecture, early childhood education, and dynamic STEM projects. The building blocks of education can begin with inspiring questions such as this one from Gadzikowski's beautiful new book, 'I noticed your tower fell over and now you're building it again. Are you doing it the same way or doing something new?' A great question for us all."

—**Frances Judd,** special projects coordinator, early childhood TESLab teacher, Bennett Day School

"*Young Architects at Play* is a user-friendly treasure for teachers, with an emphasis on both play and on learning, to encourage truly playful learning. This inspiring resource makes STEAM experiences easy to implement with lots of open-ended questions."

—**Laurie Sahn, MEd,** kindergarten teacher, The Joseph Sears School

"At last! Ann Gadzikowski's must-have book of innovative ideas emphasizing STEM-rich construction projects, finally shines a spotlight on the many benefits of introducing architecture to young children. The fifteen skillfully designed and beautifully illustrated projects with suggestions for materials, starting points, extensions and resources, will inspire educators and parents to challenge, engage, and delight their aspiring young architects."

—**Rosanne Regan Hansel,** author of *Creative Block Play: A Comprehensive Guide to Learning through Building*

Young Architects at Play

Other Redleaf Press books by Ann Gadzikowski

Robotics for Young Children: STEM Activities and Simple Coding

Creating a Beautiful Mess: Ten Essential Play Experiences
for a Joyous Childhood

Challenging Exceptionally Bright Children in Early Childhood Classrooms

Story Dictation: A Guide for Early Childhood Professionals

Young Architects at **Play**

STEM Activities
for Young Children

Ann Gadzikowski

Redleaf Press®
www.redleafpress.org
800-423-8309

Published by Redleaf Press
10 Yorkton Court
St. Paul, MN 55117
www.redleafpress.org

First edition 2020
Senior editor: Melissa York
Managing editor: Douglas Schmitz
Art director: Renee Hammes
Cover design: Michelle Lee Lagerroos
Cover photograph (bottom): iStock.com/FatCamera
Interior design: Percolator
Typeset in Abril Text
Printed in the United States of America
28 27 26 25 24 23 22 21   1 2 3 4 5 6 7 8

The book covers on pages 53, 78, and 109 are reproduced with the permission of the publisher, Penguin Random House, New York, NY.

Library of Congress Cataloging-in-Publication Data

Names: Gadzikowski, Ann, author.
Title: Young architects at play : STEM activities for young children / by Ann Gadzikowski.
Description: First edition. | St. Paul, MN : Redleaf Press, 2021. | Includes bibliographical references. | Summary: "When we see children's construction play through the lens of architecture, we are able to support and extend children's learning on all four STEM subjects: science, technology, engineering, and math. *Young Architects at Play* is a guide for both teachers and parents and includes a diverse variety of activities and resources"—Provided by publisher.
Identifiers: LCCN 2020010357 (print) | LCCN 2020010358 (ebook) | ISBN 9781605547008 (paperback) | ISBN 9781605547015 (ebook)
Subjects: LCSH: Early childhood education—Activity programs. | Science—Study and teaching (Early childhood) | Play.
Classification: LCC LB1139.35.A37 G34 2021 (print) | LCC LB1139.35.A37 (ebook) | DDC 372.21—dc23
LC record available at https://lccn.loc.gov/2020010357
LC ebook record available at https://lccn.loc.gov/2020010358

Printed on acid-free paper

To the many talented and caring teachers and staff members
at Preschool of the Arts in Madison, Wisconsin

Contents

Acknowledgments

The winter conference of the North American Reggio Emilia Alliance took place in Madison, Wisconsin in March 2019. My job as a conference volunteer and chair of the local Wonder of Learning exhibit was to drive the featured speakers from place to place. These honored visitors included Marina Castagnetti, an Italian author and educator who worked with Loris Malaguzzi in creating the acclaimed preschools and infant-toddler centers of Reggio Emilia; Nunzia Franzese, a rising pedagogista in Reggio Emilia; and Jane McCall, their expert interpreter.

On their one free afternoon in Madison, I asked where I might take them. They said they wanted to see the work of the Wisconsin-born architect Frank Lloyd Wright. So we spent a lovely afternoon visiting landmark Wright buildings, including the First Unitarian Society Meeting House, with its striking geometric windows and vaulted roof.

As we visited these beautiful buildings and talked about our work with children, I was impressed by the many similarities between designing a building and educating a child—two important endeavors that require an understanding of both art and science. The experience deepened my interest in exploring the synchronicities between architecture and early childhood education. I'm grateful to Marina, Nunzia, and Jane for sharing that reflective afternoon with me.

I'm also grateful to the children, families, teachers, and staff members of Preschool of the Arts in Madison for deepening my knowledge and experience of Reggio-inspired practices. In particular, this book's emphasis on the use of provocations in inspiring children's curiosity is largely informed by my experience at Preschool of the Arts.

I also thank the children, families, teachers, and staff members at School for Little Children in Evanston, Illinois. Many of the activities in this book were developed and tested in the science, technology, engineering, and math (STEM) enrichment classes I teach there with three- and four-year-olds.

I've always enjoyed block play—first as a child and later as a teacher. My work at Northwestern University's Center for Talent Development (CTD) sparked an even deeper interest in the field of architecture and its relevance to early childhood curriculum. I'm grateful to my CTD colleagues Susan Corwith, Beth Dirkes, and Leslie Morrison for their support, encouragement, and collaboration in developing and piloting architecture courses for young children, such as Blocks and Blueprints and LEGO Metropolis.

Many thanks to the wonderful people at Redleaf Press, who continue to champion my work and my books. It's such an honor to be able to call myself a Redleaf author. I'm grateful to Meredith Burks, Heidi Hogg, and Melissa York for their roles in creating this book. I'm especially thankful for the opportunity to work with the amazing Angela Wiechmann on the editing process.

As always, I'm grateful for the love and encouragement of my friends and family. Thank you for helping me lug my bags and boxes of blocks from place to place, and thank you for listening to my dreams.

Prólogo / Foreword

Jorge Raedó, director, Osa Menor Arts Education for Children and Youth

Bogotá, 20 de febrero de 2020

El libro de Ann es agradable, sencillo y útil. Está escrito con sus años de experiencia como profesora de jardín de infancia, tras muchas horas de observación, experimentación y estudio de la realidad infantil.

Ann ha probado diversos materiales y procesos inspirados en la arquitectura y el diseño: volúmenes geométricos, palos, bloques y todo aquello que nos permite levantar estructuras, construir ambientes, esbozar mundos urbanos con calles, casas, parques... maquetas y escenografías que permiten al niño tejer narraciones simbólicas donde puede construir sus deseos, voluntades, temores... juegos simbólicos para tejer la red social donde el niño, desde que nace, es.

Cuando digo que hay proyectos que abordan la infancia, la arquitectura* y la educación hablo de una extensa gama de profesionales que trabajan desde diferentes enfoques con diversos objetivos.

El mapa de los proyectos que aúnan infancia, arquitectura y educación podría ser así:

- *Aprendizaje de la arquitectura como un lenguaje del arte.* Igual que los niños aprenden música, pintura, teatro... aprenden arquitectura. Cursos y talleres que introducen a los pequeños el ABC de la disciplina: estructura,

*Cuando digo "Arquitectura" incluyo Diseño, Urbanismo, Paisaje.

Bogota, February 20, 2020

Ann's book *Young Architects at Play* is pleasant, simple, and useful. Her writing reflects her experience as a teacher of young children—her many hours of observation of children's play, her experimentation as a teacher, and her study of children's reality.

Ann has tested various materials and processes inspired by architecture and design: geometric volumes, sticks, blocks, and everything that allows children to raise up structures, build environments, and sketch out urban worlds with streets, houses, parks—models and scenographies that allow children to weave symbolic narratives where they can build their desires, wills, and fears ... symbolic games for weaving the social network where the child is from birth.

When I say that there are projects that address childhood, architecture* and education, I speak of a wide range of professionals who work from different approaches with different objectives.

The map of the projects that combine childhood, architecture, and education could be like this:

- *Learning architecture as a language of art.* Just like children learn music, painting, and theater, they learn architecture. Courses and workshops introduce children to the ABCs of the

*When I say "architecture," I include design, urban planning, and landscape.

escala, proporción, materiales, luz y sombra, colores, programa, contexto histórico y urbano, sostenibilidad. . .

- *Procesos de diseño participativo con protagonistas infantiles en la transformación de su mundo.* ¿Cómo? Con proyectos donde los niños, con ayuda de sus maestros, profesionales del diseño, padres y comunidad estudian un problema y lo solucionan con el diseño y construcción. Por ejemplo, la transformación del patio escolar.

- *Procesos de regeneración urbana: aquellos proyectos que quieren mejorar el espacio urbano donde vive la infancia.* Por ejemplo, mejora de parques, patios de recreo, y barrios en mal estado físico y social, y reformas de edificios puntuales como colegios o bibliotecas que ayudan a transformar un sector de la ciudad.

- *Material didáctico y lúdico desde la arquitectura y el diseño.* Los más famosos para centros educativos son los de Froebel, Montessori y Reggio Emilia. Hay decenas de buenos juegos de origen lúdico como los creados por los artistas de las vanguardias artísticas del siglo XX (Ladislav Sutnar, Joaquín Torres-García, Alma Siedhoff-Buscher. . .) o las piezas de LEGO o Kapla.

- *Infraestructura educativa.* Los edificios, con los espacios interiores y exteriores que configuran, son una herramienta más para el aprendizaje de la infancia. Toda escuela infantil o colegio (el guante). . . tiene que diseñarse a partir de un proyecto

discipline: structure, scale, proportion, materials, light and shadow, colors, program, historical and urban context, sustainability, and so on.

- *Participatory design processes with children protagonists in the transformation of their world.* How? With projects where children, with the help of their teachers, design professionals, parents, and community study a problem and solve it with design and construction—for example, the transformation of the schoolyard.

- *Urban regeneration processes: projects that improve the urban space where children live.* For example, improvement of parks, playgrounds, and neighborhoods in poor physical and social condition, and updates to specific buildings, such as schools or libraries that help transform a sector of the city.

- *Educational and playful material from architecture and design.* The most famous for educational centers are those by Froebel, Montessori, and Reggio Emilia. There are dozens of good toys designed to be playful, such as those created by avant-garde artists of the twentieth century (for example, Ladislav Sutnar, Joaquín Torres-García, Alma Siedhoff-Buscher) or the pieces of LEGO or Kapla.

- *Educational infrastructure.* The buildings, with the indoor and outdoor spaces they configure, are another tool for childhood learning. Every child care program or preschool (the glove) has to be designed from a clear

pedagógico claro (la mano). Hay buenos ejemplos en el mundo, por ejemplo, las escuelas infantiles de la "estrategia" Reggio Emilia, y los nuevos colegios de Finlandia diseñados desde el principio por los arquitectos y el equipo educativo del centro.

- *Formación continua del profesorado.* Cursos, talleres, publicaciones. . . sobre el potencial educador del espacio, cómo usar un espacio determinado para cumplir con éxito el objetivo pedagógico, el uso de la arquitectura como lenguaje artístico y forma de expresión del niño, los procesos de diseño participativo. . . El profesor es clave en la educación, como el agricultor es clave en el campo.

Ann habla en su libro de experiencias incluídas en este mapa. Ella habla de varios tipos de materiales didácticos en madera dándonos consejos para su uso. También explica el buen uso del espacio para motivar y ordenar la acción del niño, de procesos de diseño participativo desarrollados en varios días, de construcción y destrucción de mundos como forma de expresión. . . es decir, como forma de construcción del mundo personal del niño y del grupo social al que pertenece. Una buena escuela infantil ayuda a mejorar la comunidad que la acoge, como demostró María Montessori hace décadas. Finalmente, el propio libro de Ann es material de la formación continua del profesorado.

La niña explora su entorno inmediato: sillas, cojines, lápices de colores, hojas en blanco, luces y sombras que entran por las

pedagogical project (the hand). There are good examples in the world, for example, the children's schools of the Reggio Emilia "approach" and the new schools in Finland designed from the beginning by the architects and the educational team of the center.

- *Continuous teacher training.* This includes courses, workshops, and publications on the educational potential of space, how to use a specific space to successfully achieve the pedagogical objective, the use of architecture as an artistic language and a child's way of expression, participatory design processes, and so on. The teacher is key in education, just as the farmer is key in agriculture.

Ann speaks in her book of experiences included in this map. She talks about various types of wooden educational materials, giving us tips for using them. She also explains the good use of space to motivate and order the child's action, participatory design processes developed over several days, construction and destruction of worlds as a way of expression, that is, as a way of building the personal worlds of the children and the social groups to which they belong. A good early childhood school helps improve the community that hosts it, as Maria Montessori demonstrated decades ago. Finally, Ann's book is material for continuous teacher training.

The child explores her immediate surroundings: chairs, cushions, colored pencils, blank sheets, lights and shadows that enter through the windows, stones, branches, flowers, outside air, sand, water, heat and

ventanas, piedras, ramas, flores, aire exterior, arena, agua, calor y frío. . . observa, toca y huele, capta las formas con sus dedos, las agrupa, relaciona con líneas, construye un mapa, topografía de formas que activa su imaginación. Surgen historias, personajes, relaciones, intercambios y choques de deseos, conflictos que ocasionan resoluciones, cambios de formas y evolución de la topografía y las historias imaginadas. Otros niños se unen al juego y se multiplican las capas de significado.

La niña crece, se hace profesora en una escuela de primera infancia y juega, investiga, estudia, invita a niñas y niños a jugar y explorar el mundo con ella. . . invita a otros adultos a intercambiar conocimientos, a probar esto y aquello, qué funciona mejor, qué nos divierte más. El espacio cambia con nosotros, nosotros cambiamos con el espacio.

cold, and so on. She observes, touches and smells, captures the shapes with her fingers, groups them, relates lines, builds a map, a topography of forms that activates her imagination. Stories, characters, relationships, exchanges, and clashes of desires arise, conflicts that cause resolutions, changes of forms, and the evolution of topography and imagined stories. Other children join the game and multiply the layers of meaning.

The child grows up, becomes an early childhood teacher, and plays, researches, studies, invites the children to play and explore the world with her. She invites other adults to exchange knowledge, to try this and that, what works best, what amuses us. Space changes with us as we change with space.

Why Architecture?

Preschool teacher Amanda and her coteacher Kelly lead their class of three-year-olds onto the playground. It's a mild spring day, and the smell of freshly mown grass fills the air. The children scatter in all directions. Some start digging with plastic shovels in the sandbox, and others hop on trikes and begin riding along the bike path.

Amanda and Kelly position themselves on the playground so they can see and supervise all the children. Amanda notices one child, Lucy, crouching next to the bike shed. Amanda wonders what Lucy might be doing. Amanda moves toward the bike shed and keeps a close, curious eye on Lucy.

Amanda observes Lucy first kneeling, then sitting on the ground, digging in a patch of dirt with a stick. Intrigued, Amanda wonders, "Why has this child chosen to play in this patch of dirt? If she wants to dig, why doesn't she dig in the sandbox?" But rather than interrupt Lucy's play, Amanda decides to observe Lucy to see how her play develops.

Amanda notices that Lucy doesn't seem upset or lonely. In fact, the expression on Lucy's face is happy and relaxed. She seems focused. She also collects additional sticks and other small objects that happen to be nearby: a few large leaves, a smooth stone, a handful of flat wood chips. Lucy carefully arranges these small items on the patch of dirt. Next she takes a handful of twigs and pushes them into the soft dirt. She then props a layer of flat leaves across the top of the sticks.

Amanda wonders what Lucy might be building. But again, she does not want to interrupt. Instead, she takes a few steps closer to get a better view of the work.

As Amanda nears, Lucy take a small round stone and places it at the front of her structure. She then looks up at her teacher and smiles. Lucy points to the stone.

"She lives here," she says.

"Oh, are you making a house?" asks Amanda.

Lucy's face lights up. "Yes!" she says. "It's a house. I'm building it."

————

In this scenario the teacher, Amanda, observes a child at play and wonders about the meaning behind it. Like many reflective teachers, Amanda is curious about the choices children make during play. In this case she wonders why a child would choose to dig in the dirt and build a structure using stray objects found on the ground, especially when a sandbox and a variety of digging toys are available nearby.

After reading this scenario, you may have been curious too. Perhaps you have your own ideas about the reasons behind this child's choices. Maybe you

Building a house out of blocks is almost a universal play experience.

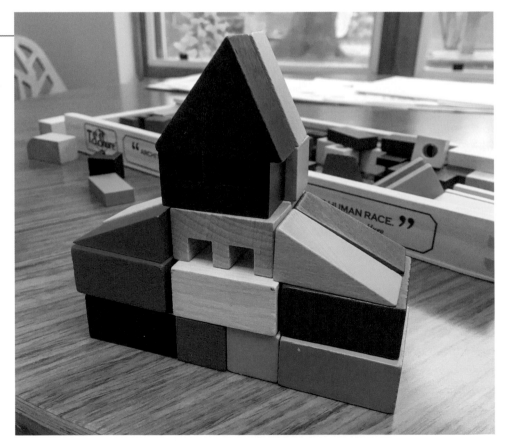

can recall your own experiences playing outdoors as a child. Do you remember the allure of building something out of sticks and other natural materials you picked up from the ground?

Children seem to universally enjoy building, whether with natural objects, blocks, or other materials. Human nature and the drive to create feed the desire to build.

Children also often create narratives around the structures they build. In this scenario Lucy is not only building a structure but creating a pretend story in her head. She uses a stone to represent the character who lives in this little building.

This is a single, ordinary moment in the relationship between a teacher and a child—seemingly nothing more than a brief exchange about a pile of sticks and leaves. Yet it contains many elements of best practices in early childhood education: an observant and supportive teacher, a curious child engaged in play, a construction project utilizing open-ended materials or "loose parts," and the narration of a story that gives meaning to the child's play.

What Is Architecture?

As an early childhood educator, I am fascinated by children's construction play. I have a deep appreciation for how it allows children to develop cognitive skills, express creativity, and add complex layers of story and meaning.

In my work with children and teachers, I've found that architecture is the bridge that connects these ideas. Architecture is the art, science, and process of planning, designing, and constructing buildings. The word *architecture* can refer to this process as well as the buildings that result from it. In this book I will focus on *architecture* as a creative process.

We often associate architecture with famous architects and complex buildings and structures. But architecture gives us vocabulary to talk about the buildings and structures all around us. You likely have a roof over your head right now as you read this page of words. Understanding architecture helps us better notice what architects call "the built environment": houses, apartment buildings, and other structures as well as roads and bridges.

As you will discover in this book, architecture also gives us examples, both real and imagined, that inspire and provoke exciting construction projects in early childhood classrooms. As a teacher, I believe thinking and learning about architecture has significantly enhanced my ability to support children's construction play and deepen their learning experiences.

Architecture and Children

The child who pokes sticks in the dirt and builds a home for her rock is an architect. Every child who constructs a house out of sticks or stones or blocks or LEGO is an architect. Architecture is demonstrated every day in children's play across the globe.

So why don't we see the topic of architecture included in early childhood education? Why is it almost invisible when it comes to how and what children learn?

We usually only find courses and curriculum bearing the title of "Architecture" at the college level. And out of the 1.5 million bibliographic records in the Educational Resources Information Center, only *two* records are related to teaching young children about architecture. Both involve projects with school-age children (kindergarten through grade five) (Hollingsworth 1993; Luera and Hong 2003). There are *zero* articles documenting any connection between the topic of architecture and children five and younger.

It seems that architecture is not intended for children. However, young children usually already have an intuitive sense of architecture. More simply, they understand that every building has a purpose. They understand that homes are built to provide shelter. Schools are built so we can come together and learn. Stores are built so people can buy food and other things they need. And hospitals are built so we can take care of people who are hurt or ill. Children realize there is a clear sense of purpose in the various buildings and structures in our communities—a sense that form follows function.

Therefore, there are many developmentally appropriate ways that the study of architecture can begin in early childhood. For example, children may look at pictures of different kinds of buildings, visit buildings in their neighborhoods, and talk about why and how we build. In turn these architecture-related activities can inspire children to develop new ideas through block and construction play. Talking and thinking about architectural features, such as doors and windows, can also add complexity and interest to children's construction projects.

Constructivism and Architecture

Constructivism is a theory of cognitive development. It is centered on the idea that children learn through direct physical experience, through play, and through their interactions with their environment. This approach to early learning, as articulated by theorists Jean Piaget and Lev Vygotsky, emphasizes the importance of children's physical, sensory experiences with the world around them.

No doubt construction play is a true form of constructivist learning. Whether with blocks, toys, or other materials, construction play is at the core of developmentally appropriate practice.

As a constructivist early childhood educator, I believe architecture provides an important connection bridging young children's play to the real-world skills and knowledge they will develop as productive adults. Architecture engages all four STEM content areas: science, technology, engineering, and math.

Construction play and architecture-inspired activities also develop important spatial skills. This is especially true when children represent their ideas using three-dimensional tools (blocks, loose parts, and construction toys) as well as two-dimensional tools (drawing, writing, and mapping).

Construction play is at the core of developmentally appropriate practice.

At the same time, architecture also provides opportunities for creative and artistic expression, language development, and literacy development. Ludwig Mies van der Rohe, the German American regarded as a pioneer of modernist architecture, is credited with asserting that "architecture is a language" (Domus 2016).

This phrase calls to mind the words of Loris Malaguzzi, founder of the renowned infant-toddler centers and preschools of Reggio Emilia, Italy. Malaguzzi explored the concept of "the hundred languages of children." He wrote, "The child has a hundred languages, a hundred thoughts, a hundred ways of thinking, of playing, of speaking. A hundred, always a hundred ways of listening, of marveling, of loving, a hundred joys, for singing, for understanding, a hundred worlds to discover, a hundred worlds to invent, a hundred worlds to dream" (Malaguzzi 1993, 3).

It's highly unlikely that van der Rohe and Malaguzzi ever met, yet their ideas beautifully align. Architecture is indeed a language—one of the hundred children use to express themselves. This language can be artfully expressed even on a small scale, as represented in construction play and architecture explorations in the preschool classroom.

Benefits of Architectural Play

Simply put, architectural play supports children's capacity to learn. Here's how the open-ended and creative play experiences described throughout this book support healthy brain development:

- Construction play is meaningful. When children build freely from their own imagination, creating houses and other structures, they connect their prior knowledge with new inventions and experiences. Making meaningful connections stimulates networks in the brain associated with logical thinking, metacognition, and creativity.

- Construction play is actively engaging. The physical tasks associated with construction play—such as lifting, stacking, and balancing—activate areas of the brain associated with decision-making, executive function, and self-regulation.

- Construction play is iterative. An iterative process is one that involves repetition, experimentation, and exploration. During construction play, towers fall, roofs cave in, and walls tumble. Most children are eager to try and try again until they find success. The perseverance demonstrated during construction play engages neural networks that are associated with flexible thinking and creativity.

- Construction play is socially interactive. In most early childhood classrooms, construction play takes place in pairs and small groups. Collaboration and conversation promote plasticity in the brain that helps children develop empathy and social skills.

- Construction play is joyful. The block corner is often the loudest area of the classroom—and for good reason. Joy is noisy. The excitement of building with blocks or any material makes children laugh and call out to each other with joy. This sets the stage for a lifetime of health and well-being, as joy is associated with chemicals that are linked to enhanced memory, attention, and motivation, such as dopamine.

Physical, Tangible, and Sensory Construction Play

The value of hands-on construction play has long been embraced by leaders and thinkers, such as Piaget and German educator Friederich Fröebel, who created the first kindergarten in the early nineteenth century. More recently the value of hands-on construction play has been the focus of educators and parents who are concerned about children's screen time—the time they are engaged with tablets, smartphones, laptops, and other electronic devices.

For many children, playing in a virtual world with electronic devices has replaced some of the time they would spend playing in the real world with tangible objects. In particular, many children enjoy virtual construction games and apps, including Toca Builders and Minecraft.

Common Sense Media is a nonprofit organization that provides research and recommendations regarding technology and media. It reports that for children ages eight and younger, one-third of all screen time is on mobile devices, and between 2011 and 2017 the amount of time children spent on mobile devices tripled (Common Sense Media 2017).

While there may be many benefits to learning how to navigate digital tools, concerns about screen time have been expressed at every level of education. Constructivist educators and advocates for developmentally appropriate practice recognize that hands-on construction play—with real, tangible tools—offers cognitive, physical, and social benefits that can't be gained from a screen.

Debbie Sterling is a Stanford-trained engineer and inventor of GoldiBlox, a media company focusing on the principles of STEM. She advocates for hands-on construction play in early childhood, as it establishes a foundation of essential spatial reasoning skills (Sterling 2013).

A similar observation was made at the college level, illustrating how construction play builds real-world skills. Ron Kasprisin, architecture professor and author of *Play in Creative Problem-Solving for Planners and Architects*, advocates using tangible tools, such as cardboard, foam, and clay, as part of the design process for his architecture and urban-planning students. He writes, "My recent experiences (over the past five years or more) with undergraduate and graduate students in planning and design who have not used any methodology or tool except those related to the computer (digital technologies) have strengthened my resolve to bring back the other half, the sensual half of the creative process" (Kasprisin 2016, 206). At every level of schooling, from early childhood to college, educators and researchers are noting the importance of balancing digital learning with tangible learning.

The Theme of Home

In early childhood classrooms we may not use the word *architecture*, but we often use the word *home*. Children intuitively understand the purpose and meaning of a home. They know it is where you eat, sleep, rest, go to the bathroom. Important things happen there. A home is a place of belonging, a place for family and friends. Homes can be big or small. They can house a single family or, in the case of a tall apartment building, can house many families.

A home provides shelter, which is an essential human need. Erik Erikson's theory of human development tells us that our first task on this earth is to learn to trust. It's the foundation on which all relationships and meaningful experiences are built. A home—with a literal foundation, a sheltering roof, and a soft place to rest—is a tangible, physical representation of the trust we build from birth. A home holds us and keeps us safe in the same way that children's trusted caregivers—their parents, family members, and teachers—hold them close and protect them.

It makes sense, then, that a house is the structure children most often choose to build with construction materials. Just as children construct their knowledge of the world and build their sense of trust in others, they also build homes and houses with their hands.

The unifying theme of this book, then, is the concept of home—the most familiar sheltering structure in children's lives. The concept of home also allows for an unlimited variety of related projects and investigations into other homes: dollhouses, tree houses, doghouses, and so on.

However, when we focus on homes in our construction activities, we must be aware that this topic can be very emotional and intense for some children. When children are at school, they often think of home, and some desperately miss their homes and family. All of us long for the safety and security of our homes.

Also, intentional teachers in inclusive classrooms are aware that some children may be experiencing or have experienced homelessness or housing instability. Others may have experienced traumatic changes in their living conditions. Even an ordinary family move from one house to another can be frightening and confusing for young children. Exploring the idea of home during construction play is one way we can offer children some power and creative autonomy.

Teachers can support and facilitate construction play by "building" on children's interest in homes and houses. Provocations and open-ended questions can spark new ideas about the design and architecture of the homes

The Architecture of This Book

Throughout this book there is an emphasis on higher-order thinking and critical thinking in STEM. The structure of the chapters, and of the book as a whole, provides a path for scaffolding learning about architecture and related STEM topics.

The book is divided into two parts. In part 1 each chapter focuses on a specific type of material or tool: blocks, natural materials and loose parts, found objects and recycled materials, and wood. In part 2 we'll examine how to facilitate architectural explorations using resources such as picture books, maps, and collaborative projects.

The chapters progress from the most familiar materials and ideas to the most novel materials and challenging ideas. Likewise, the ideas and projects within each chapter are organized on a continuum, beginning with the most open-ended activities and progressing to more structured projects.

As a whole, this organization represents the way young children typically respond to construction materials. They begin with open-ended exploration and then form ideas and intentions about how the materials can be used.

Provocations

For every project in this book, you will find details about how to create provocations. *Provocation* is a term frequently used by Reggio Emilia–inspired educators to describe a display or presentation of materials that teachers intentionally arrange to "provoke" or inspire learning. A provocation often involves something children may not have encountered before—a novel item or a new combination of materials. Teachers usually assemble a provocation before the school day begins. That way the provocation will greet the children as they enter the classroom and perhaps spark conversation and excitement during the first part of the day.

For example, a provocation for a block activity might be as simple as a sequence of three unit blocks placed flat, end to end, in a row. This would perhaps invite a child to continue with the sequence and create a path or road. Another provocation might include an image of a building to inspire construction play. Perhaps a novel mix of construction toys or materials, such as domino tiles or craft sticks, might provoke new ideas for creative building.

This simple provocation, magnetic tiles and a string of holiday lights, draws children's attention to the transparency of the tiles.

A provocation can be placed in a central location in the classroom, such as on a table or a rug. As children are welcomed to the classroom at the beginning of the day or session, their attention will be drawn to the materials.

That said, a provocation does not always have to be placed in a prominent location. A small provocation can be displayed in an out-of-the-way location in the classroom. It can be a little surprise for the child or children who discover it.

Provocations ease children not only into a specific activity but also into their day. Seeing an array of interesting materials might help children who feel sad or worried when they separate from their caregivers. A provocation gives children something to look forward to and provides a space to begin playing with a friend. Engaging in play at the start of the day or session also helps support children's social development. The open-ended nature of loose parts allows each child to play at their own pace and explore their own interests. Everyone can take part.

A Final Word

I am an old-school constructivist early childhood educator inspired by Reggio Emilia. I have had the good fortune of working alongside excellent STEM educators at Northwestern University, where I learned how to introduce STEM concepts to young children using developmentally appropriate practices. This book is also informed by the Reggio Emilia–inspired practices at Preschool of the Arts in Madison, Wisconsin.

My hope is that this book will build a bridge between construction play in early childhood classrooms and the real-world experience of architecture in the daily lives of every human being. As I researched for this book, I was often reminded of the lovely British expression "Safe as houses." It means to be quite secure and trustworthy.

I hope this book will become a trusted resource for you and the children you teach.

PART 1

Materials

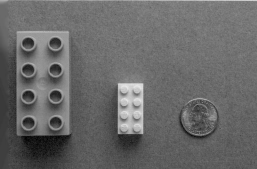

CHAPTER 1

Blocks and Construction Toys

As mentioned in the introduction, construction play is a demonstration of constructivist learning. Piaget and Vygotsky teach us that children construct knowledge through their direct experience with the environment and with other people. Constructivism relates to all kinds of active play, but it is most beautifully relevant to block play. When children build with blocks, they literally construct their knowledge of shape, size, weight, scale, balance, symmetry, gravity, and more.

In terms of learning, block play develops many of the "big ideas" of early math as defined by the Erikson Institute Early Math Collaborative: shape, spatial relationships, patterns, and measurement (Brownell et al. 2014). Block play also demonstrates all five of the characteristics associated with healthy brain development described in the research summary *Neuroscience and Learning through Play: A Review of the Evidence*, published by the LEGO Foundation (Liu et al. 2017).

In addition, building with blocks is creative expression, a demonstration and practice of architectural design concepts. Frank Lloyd Wright famously noted the relationship between his childhood experiences with blocks and his exceptional career as an architect: "The smooth cardboard triangles and maple-wood blocks were most important. All are in my fingers to this day. . . . I soon became susceptible to constructive pattern evolving in everything I saw. I learned to 'see' this way and when I did, I did not care to draw casual incidentals to Nature. I wanted to design" (Turner 2011).

Let's take a closer look at how and why block play is an integral part of early childhood education.

The Unit Block

Just as a living organism is made of individual cells, a preschooler's complex block structure is made of individual blocks. And in early childhood classrooms, the cell of constructivist play is the basic brick, also known as the unit block. It has a standardized shape and size consistent among toy and school supply products.

The standard unit block is 5.5 inches long, 2.75 inches wide, and 1.375 inches thick.

The idea that children will benefit from building with uniform blocks stems back to Fröbel, who designed a numbered series of classroom toys called "Gifts." When examined in order, each Gift is more complex than the previous one.

For example, Gift 1 is a simple ball, a sphere. Gift 2 is a set of three objects with different shapes: a sphere, a cube, and a cylinder. Gift 3 is a set of eight cube blocks, which can be assembled into a larger cube as a tangible lesson in how the whole is the sum of its parts. Gift 4 is a set of eight rectangular prism blocks. Many popular construction toys, such as LEGO, can trace their heritage back to Gift 4.

Inspired by Fröbel's Gifts, American educator Caroline Pratt designed unit blocks in the early twentieth century. Pratt was both a preschool teacher and a woodworker. She tested many different block proportions and types of wood until she came up with what she believed was the perfect design for construction play. At 5.5 inches long, 2.75 inches wide, and 1.375 inches thick, the unit block has a mathematically beautiful ratio of 1:2:4.

The third Fröbel Gift is a set of eight cube blocks.

Few play materials provide more benefit than wooden blocks. So even if your set of unit blocks is battered and worn, it's still one of the most valuable treasures in your classroom. In *The Design of Childhood: How the Material World Shapes Independent Kids*, Alexandra Lange remarks that unit blocks "always seem to be used most quickly, forcing children to assemble more idiosyncratic pieces—the squares, the right triangles—back into satisfying bricks, teaching basic principles of geometry, by the by, the same way Froebel's cubes-in-a-cube did" (Lange 2018, 31).

The Role of the Brick in Architecture

Building with unit blocks is not just a whimsical or abstract activity for children. Rather, it's a direct connection to actual construction in the real world. Just as unit blocks are essential to block play, basic bricks are essential to architecture. Take a quick glance around your community and you'll see how ubiquitous bricks are in the design and construction of buildings.

Masonry is a type of construction that uses stone or concrete bricks, blocks, and tiles. Bricks have a standard size and shape in masonry construction. Like unit blocks, they are rectangular prisms. Mortar, a binding adhesive, is used to hold the bricks together. Bricks are often made of clay, not wood.

The term *brickwork* is used to describe the patterns and processes used to lay the brick.

Why are bricks so essential? As a teacher, I often ask children, "Would you rather build a house out of unit blocks or cubes? Why?" So I now ask you, my reader, a similar question: "Why is a rectangular prism better for building than a square cube?"

You might begin by commenting that a rectangular prism has elongated planes, or sides. In contrast a cube has square planes with less surface area. This is key. The elongated planes provide more surface to spread mortar. And due to its longer length, a rectangular prism also lends itself better to an alternating pattern than does a cube. Staggering the bricks in their placement creates a much stronger wall than placing them in direct alignment.

The concept of the brick, a rectangular prism, is important in both architecture and block play.

Other Types of Blocks

Wooden unit blocks are practically perfect for any kind of preschool block play. However, there are certainly other options and block systems to inspire architectural play.

Wooden plank blocks, such as KEVA or KAPLA blocks, share many features with unit blocks. Each plank is a standard and uniform size and weight, though smaller and lighter than unit blocks. Plank blocks can be used on either the floor or a table. Because they are smaller than unit blocks, plank blocks require greater dexterity to manipulate and are better suited for older preschoolers and kindergarteners.

Plank blocks are smaller and lighter than unit blocks.

Cube blocks are less common than rectangular prism blocks. The different shape offers varied opportunities for building. A set of simple wooden cube blocks is reminiscent of the original Fröbel Gifts from the nineteenth century. And yet many children today are drawn to cube blocks, either wooden or foam, because they are inspired by digital games such as Minecraft. Cubes are the literal building blocks for structures and even characters in these games.

Magnetic tiles and blocks are also popular construction toys. Some brands include Magna-Tiles, PicassoTiles, and Tegu Blocks. Interestingly, building with magnetic toys is both very easy and very difficult for children. It's easy because the magnets snap the blocks together, keeping them connected without having to worry about balance and symmetry. On the other hand, if the magnets aren't properly aligned—say, if a positive pole meets another positive pole—the blocks will snap apart or shift their position.

If you have magnetic building toys in your learning environment, it's important to talk with children about how magnets work. This helps scaffold their understanding so they can learn how to take advantage of the power of the magnets.

For example, if something unexpected or frustrating happens to a child building with magnetic construction toys, turn it into a teachable moment. Begin by asking open-ended questions to gauge what the child already understands about magnets. You might say, "I see the roof of your house snapped apart and fell down. I wonder why that happened. What do you think?"

Perhaps the child will say the word *magnet* and show some understanding of how magnets work. In that case help her explore, through trial and error, how turning the block around will make a stronger bond.

Or perhaps the child has no experience with, or understanding of, magnets. Then it might be helpful to use a pair of plain horseshoe or bar magnets, with the poles labeled and visible, to show the child how magnets can attract and repel each other. Once a basic concept is in place, you can apply it to how the blocks attract and repel.

LEGO Blocks

LEGO is a very popular block system. Invented in 1932 by Danish toymaker Ole Kirk Cristiansen, LEGO blocks are colorful, come in many sizes and shapes, and are relatively inexpensive.

Also popular is Duplo, LEGO's chubby cousin. Duplo blocks are recommended for children under age three and for children new to LEGO construction. Because Duplo blocks are larger than LEGO blocks, they are easier to manipulate with little hands, and they don't pose choking hazards.

Both LEGO and Duplo blocks offer a different experience than wooden blocks. Wooden blocks rest on each other, using only the force of gravity, while LEGO blocks have an interlocking design that firmly snaps together. It's important to stress, however, that due to this interlocking system, LEGO blocks can't provide the same level of challenge and creativity as wooden unit blocks. Children develop fine-motor and cognitive skills as they learn to balance and align wooden unit blocks in strong and symmetrical patterns.

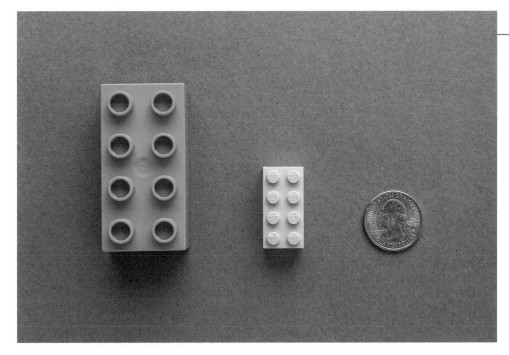

A Duplo brick, shown here in green, is much larger and easier to manipulate than a LEGO brick, shown here in yellow.

As supplemental construction toys, though, LEGO blocks inspire nearly endless creativity for building, design, and construction. Because of their versatility, they are well regarded as a learning and modeling tool among many professional architects.

The LEGO House—a children's museum and play space in Billund, Denmark—features an interactive exhibit called "6 Bricks Factory." The exhibit demonstrates how even a small number of classic LEGO bricks can be arranged in many creative ways. In fact, mathematician Søren Eilers has determined that six LEGO bricks can be arranged in 915,103,765 combinations (Higgins 2017).

Blocks and Deconstruction

Nearly every block construction activity turns into a deconstruction activity at some point—whether by intent or accident. As we discussed in the introduction, deconstruction provides many opportunities for emotional and social development as well as logical and analytical thinking.

Fröbel's Gift 3, the eight cubes, demonstrates how deconstructing a block structure is a form of early mathematical learning. The eight cubes stack into a larger cube and are stored in a box shaped like a cube. Because the larger cube is made of parts, it can be constructed and deconstructed.

Fröbel's blocks suggest a parallel between deconstruction in block play and decomposition in mathematics. To decompose numbers means to break them down into their subparts. Number decomposition is typically taught in kindergarten. So while preschool children might not be ready to learn about numbers decomposition, hands-on experiences with blocks can provide foundations for computational thinking.

The Block Corner

To be licensed and accredited, child care and preschool classrooms are often required to provide space for block play. There are many practical considerations when choosing where and how to set up your space.

The "block corner" is a common feature in many early educational environments. A corner of the classroom is quite often the logical choice, as it will keep the block area away from the regular flow of traffic. A carpet or rug with a smooth low pile will help dampen the loud sounds of the blocks when they fall to the floor.

A classroom set of unit blocks usually includes fifty to one hundred blocks. Store them on open shelves that are labeled with a tracing or image of each shape. This gives children easy access to select specific sizes and shapes and will also help during cleanup time. It will become yet another deconstruction learning opportunity as the children practice observing and sorting three-dimensional shapes.

The block corner can be one of the most beautiful and interesting areas of a classroom.

BUILD A HOME FOR A FAVORITE TOY

The design of a home is influenced by the needs and movements of the people—or toys—living there. Building a home for a favorite toy is a wonderful introduction to some of the core concepts of architecture. A child who may not ordinarily be interested in playing with blocks can likely be persuaded to create a cozy home for a little toy. And a child who already builds with blocks may enjoy a new, purposeful challenge.

Materials
The materials for this project are simple: unit blocks and small people or animal toys. Preferably, the toy figures should be no taller than 5.5 inches, the length of a unit block.

Provocations and Invitations
Place a bin of small toy figures in the block corner. One-on-one or in a small group, invite children to select a favorite toy from the bin. (You could also invite the children to bring a toy from home.) Ask the children, "Where does this little friend live? Does it need a home?" At the beginning of playtime, invite the children to use the unit blocks to build a home for the toy.

Considerations
Beyond the initial invitation, children will probably not need much assistance to begin building a home for their toy. Teachers may need to facilitate the sharing and distribution of blocks.

Big Ideas and Open-Ended Questions
As children build, ask open-ended questions that draw their attention to the characteristics of a home or house:

"What kind of home do you think this toy needs?"

"How big should it be? How do you know?"

"How will you build a home for the toy?"

"What do you think you need to do first?"

"What do you think you need to do next?"

"Which blocks will you use?"

A home built for a toy may or may not have a roof. Children may prefer to leave the roof open so they can still see and play with the toys inside.

"What shapes do you need?"

"How will you make the house strong and safe?"

"What are the parts of your house?"

"Do you need walls? What about a roof? Do you need doors? What about windows?"

"How will your toy go in and out of this house?"

"What will your toy do in its house?"

"Is this a house where friends can come and visit? Where will they stay?"

Next Steps

To extend learning and play, invite children to have their toys visit each other's houses. Children may also enjoy making roads or pathways between houses. Blocks or paper could be used to make roads.

ROADS AND BRIDGES

The roads and bridges that connect our homes are an important part of what architects and engineers call the "built environment." Constructing roads and bridges with blocks challenges children to use spatial reasoning in new and different ways. When children connect their structures, they collaborate and gain experience using language and social skills.

Materials

In addition to unit blocks, you will need toy cars and trucks, preferably one to two inches wide. To represent water, you will need strips of blue construction paper, about two to three inches wide.

Provocations and Invitations

Adding a basket of toy vehicles to the block area will often lead to the spontaneous building of roads and bridges. You can also wait until children have built several structures or houses, then introduce the vehicles as a method of transportation between the various buildings. As children roll the toys across the floor, ask, "I see that car is moving fast. Does it need a road?" If a vehicle encounters an obstacle in its path, suggest building a bridge to travel over the obstacle. Strips of blue paper can be used to represent rivers, and children can be invited to build bridges over the rivers. The blue paper can be laid on the floor at the start of the play period or added later, after the construction play has begun.

Considerations

Children will need a large, open area on the floor to build roads and bridges. You may need to move some furniture temporarily to make room.

When children work on connecting a bridge to a road, they may notice that they need some kind of ramp to provide their vehicle with a smooth transition from road to bridge. Unit block sets usually include several different kinds of triangular prisms that can be used as ramps. Let the children figure out which block will work best as a ramp, but be ready to help support their experimentation and discovery. You might ask, "I see your car needs a way to drive onto the bridge. What kind of block could you add in that spot?"

Big Ideas and Open-Ended Questions

As children build roads and bridges, ask questions that draw their attention to the design features of these types of structures:

"What kind of road do you need? Smooth or bumpy? Straight or curved?"

"How will you build your road?"

"What kinds of blocks do you need to make your road?"

"How will you begin?"

"Here's a river. What can you do to make your road go over the river?"

"Do you need a bridge? Have you ever gone over a bridge? What was that like?"

"What are the parts of a bridge?"

"What holds the bridge up?"

"How tall do you want your bridge to be?"

"How can you make your bridge very strong?"

"What can you do to make sure your bridge is flat and straight?"

Next Steps

The process of building roads and bridges with blocks provides natural opportunities to talk with children about measurement. Ask questions that focus children's attention on the importance of measuring.

For example, as children build a bridge across a paper river, ask, "How long will you make your bridge?" Children can measure their bridge by how many blocks they used ("This bridge is two blocks long"), or you could show them how to use a ruler and more standard units of measurement.

Children will learn through play that a long bridge requires additional supports. Again, ask questions that draw their attention to these design features: "I see this bridge has some extra blocks holding up the middle. How did you know these blocks were important?"

TOWERS AND APARTMENT BUILDINGS

Not all children live in traditional single-family homes. Children who live in multifamily homes and apartment buildings will enjoy creating structures that mirror their own familiar environment. Children who live in traditional single-family houses will benefit from learning about different kinds of homes.

Materials

You will need unit blocks, small people and animal figures, and wooden or pressboard planks. If you find that your collection of classroom blocks is not large enough for creating a variety of interesting and complex structures, try adding a few flat wooden or pressboard planks. Children can use these flat pieces for floors and foundations. I recommend rectangular pieces one to two feet in width and length and about one inch thick. Make sure the edges are smooth and will not cause scrapes or splinters.

Provocations and Invitations

Illustrations and photographs of different kinds of homes can be used as provocations that inspire children to build a wide variety of creative structures. You may want to provide photos of multifamily homes and apartment buildings from your community. I also recommend the following picture books:

Home by Carson Ellis (2015)

If You Lived Here by Giles Laroche (2011)

Windows by Julia Denos (2017)

Houses and Homes by Ann Morris (1995)

You Belong Here by M. H. Clark (2016)

Considerations

Unit blocks rarely cause injuries, but whenever children build tall towers out of blocks, make sure there's enough space around the structures for a safe "fall zone." If children build them too close together, blocks might fall on children or knock over other structures in progress.

Many children enjoy the challenge of building tall towers.

If you are using very large, heavy blocks, such as hollow wooden blocks, help children choose a building site that is a safe distance from where other children are playing on the floor. Very large blocks can also be used outdoors.

Big Ideas and Open-Ended Questions

Building larger and taller structures inspires children to solve more complex engineering problems. Constructing a tall tower of blocks requires a strong and steady base. The blocks must be balanced and aligned carefully to keep the tower from toppling over. Mistakes are opportunities for learning.

Ask questions and make observations that draw children's attention to the architectural features of towers and other large buildings:

"How will you make your building taller?"

"Which blocks work well for tall towers? Why?"

"How is building a tall tower different from building a short, little house?"

"Who lives in this building?"

"How will the people get from floor to floor?"

"I see that you put a foundation of large flat blocks at the base of your structure. Why did you choose to build it that way?"

"I noticed that your tower fell over and now you're building it again. Are you doing it the same way, or are you doing something new?"

Next Steps

Young children often become captivated by the idea of building a tower that reaches very high, perhaps even all the way to the ceiling. A wonderful example of this fascination is documented in the film *Thinking Big: Extending Emergent Curriculum Projects* (Felstiner, Pelo, and Carter 1999).

One of the great ideas demonstrated by the teachers in the film is inviting the children to build a tower on the surface of a mirror. A shatterproof acrylic mirror was placed flat on the floor. The children were invited to build on top of it with blocks. The children were amazed by the way the reflection seemed to depict the tower "growing down" as they built upward. Adding mirrors to construction play often adds surprising new perspectives and ideas.

CHAPTER 2

Natural Materials and Loose Parts

Children have been playing and building with natural materials such as sticks, stones, and leaves since long before scholars began studying child development. In fact, these natural materials are literally the foundation of architectural history.

Early humans learned to build homes in the same way young children learn to build play structures—by piecing together natural materials found in their immediate environment. Evidence of one of the first known human-built homes was discovered at Terra Amata in France. More than four hundred thousand years ago, a tribe of hunter-gatherers constructed an oval hut by pushing sapling branches into the ground and reinforcing the walls with a ring of stones (Tattersall 2013). The construction techniques of these early humans are remarkably similar to those used by the little girl in our opening scenario in the introduction, who built a miniature home out of twigs and rocks.

The Timeless Appeal of Natural Materials

Today families and schools often have access to a wide variety of colorful manufactured construction toys. So why are children still drawn to natural materials such as stones, sticks, and leaves? There are two important reasons why.

First, children enjoy the open-ended nature of "loose parts." Children can manipulate, control, and arrange these materials in an endless variety of patterns and combinations. There are no rules or instruction manuals for how to play with a stick. Each child is free to invent their own way of playing, building, and pretending. This is beautifully illustrated in Antoinette Portis's (2007) picture book *Not a Stick*, in which the main character pretends that her stick is any number of exciting props, such as a fishing pole, a sword, or a paintbrush.

Second, children enjoy playing with raw materials found outdoors because they have an intuitive fascination with the natural world. Even very young children seem to understand that the odds and ends found outdoors—parts of plants, sticks and stones, and the earth itself—are special and unique. Children don't need to be told that nature is beautiful; they can see and sense it for themselves each time they go outdoors: sunlight reflected off a body of water, multicolored plants, the sky at sunset, and all the surprising smells and textures around them. Most young children are eager to experience the gifts from Mother Nature.

Our job as teachers, caregivers, and parents is to make sure children have the opportunity to play outside as often as possible. Richard Louv, author of the acclaimed book *Last Child in the Woods*: *Saving Our Children from Nature-Deficit Disorder*, is an outspoken advocate for outdoor play. Louv writes that "just as children need good nutrition and adequate sleep, they may very well need contact with nature" (Louv 2008, 3).

Playing and building with natural materials engages children's senses with a variety of colors, textures, and shapes.

Sensory Experiences with Loose Parts and Natural Materials

Young children learn through their senses—smell, touch, sight, sound, and even taste. Piaget identified "sensorimotor" exploration as a significant stage in cognitive development. When we observe how children play with loose parts such as stones, shells, twigs, and bark, we see a variety of these behaviors. These sensory experiences are quite typical of toddlers and young preschoolers. All children, though, will display these types of sensory-based play behaviors, especially in new environments and during first encounters with novel materials.

Children often begin with sensory exploration, such as touching, holding, smelling, and perhaps even tasting the object. (This is when close supervision is necessary for safety, especially with children under age three.) Natural materials have a complex variety of smells, textures, colors, and patterns that stimulate the brain in ways manufactured materials cannot.

One of the most interesting sensory differences between natural and manufactured materials is their smell. Children are usually very quick to notice this. A basket of acorns, especially those recently foraged, has a distinctly different smell from, say, a plastic doll or a digital tablet.

While the aroma of natural materials isn't always pleasant, it is invariably a part of the learning experience. And research has shown that among the five senses, smell is the most pronounced in young children.

Another set of sensory behaviors we often see in young children is gathering and collecting, which is a form of touch. Children will often collect natural items in their hands, in pockets, or in buckets. They are especially excited when there is a large number of stones, shells, or sticks to touch, hold, manipulate, and gather.

When children play with a large quantity of items—more than ten, more than twenty, maybe even more than one hundred—they are able to manipulate the items in an endless variety of ways. Children are eager to carry, pour, sort, line up, and spread out items in creative configurations and patterns.

Open-ended sensory exploration of natural materials sets the stage for later learning in STEM subject areas. Through play, children build a foundation for exciting and challenging mathematic and scientific concepts, such as volume, classification, and conservation.

Pretend Play with Natural Materials

When preschool and school-age children build outdoors with natural materials, they frequently engage in pretend play, especially when playing together socially. A handful of colorful rocks becomes pirates' treasure. A pile of mud and stones, carefully shaped and patted into a mound, becomes a birthday cake. In many cases natural materials build large, nearly life-size structures perfect for pretend play.

A wonderful example of children's pretend play with natural materials is represented in Alice McLerran's (1991) picture book *Roxaboxen*, illustrated by Barbara Cooney. It is based on the true story of a group of children who create their own pretend town out of natural materials (e.g., rocks, sand, and thorny ocotillo sticks) as well as found objects (e.g., wooden crates and bits of broken dishes). In *Roxaboxen* the children create their homes by arranging stones in rows to establish the boundaries that represent streets and the walls of their houses. Many of the architectural features, such as roofs, are completely imaginary.

This home for toys is inspired by Alice McLerran's *Roxaboxen*, the story of children who made a pretend town out of loose parts and found objects.

This rich mix of actual objects and pretend features represents the ways many children build and create larger-scale architecture with loose parts and natural materials. Natural materials are often too small to create a larger structure that is stable and complete enough for pretend play. Rather, children use these materials to create arrangements that suggest and represent walls and roads of pretend structures large enough for them to play in. They essentially create maps of their imagination and build their own environment for make-believe play.

Architectural Play and Natural Materials

Children are more likely to build complete structures when working on a small scale. For instance, they will often add walls, roofs, and other architectural features to miniature houses made out of sticks and rocks. The open-endedness of loose parts inspires creativity and provides opportunities for problem solving.

When given ample opportunities to experiment through trial and error, children will learn that poking sticks into the soil makes for stronger walls than simply laying sticks on the surface on the ground. Aspiring architects will also discover that flat stones can be stacked, and that the larger, heavier stones work best at the bottom, providing a solid foundation for the home, close to the earth. Adding a roof to a structure is another difficult yet fascinating engineering challenge they will face. Children may find that large leaves or pieces of bark are flat and light enough for a roof.

Loose Parts in the Classroom

Lisa Daly and Miriam Beloglovsky are the authors of the essential reference on loose parts: the award-winning book *Loose Parts: Inspiring Play in Young Children* (2014). They have also written several additional books, including *Loose Parts 2: Inspiring Play for Infants and Toddlers* (2016), *Loose Parts 3: Inspiring Culturally Sustainable Environments* (2018), and *Loose Parts 4: Inspiring 21st-Century Learning* (2020).

Daly and Beloglovsky note that architect Simon Nicholson originally coined the term "loose parts." He observed that "in any environment, both the degree of inventiveness and creativity, and the possibility of discovery, are directly proportional to the number of variables in it" (Nicholson 1971, 30). For example, for a child building outdoors with sticks, the variables include the weather, the condition of the soil, and the shape and size of the sticks themselves.

A preschool classroom presents fewer environmental variables than does the great outdoors, yet we can still provide open-ended play and construction opportunities. Collections of natural materials can be brought indoors and offered to children in sensory tables or in baskets on the floor or at tables.

If you wish to bring loose parts into your early childhood classroom, you must take care to ensure the materials are safe for young children. For example, avoid items with sharp edges (e.g., pointed sticks or pine needles) and small items that might be choking hazards (e.g., small stones). Here are some examples of natural materials that can be used for loose-part play:

- rocks, stones, and pebbles
- sticks and twigs
- shells
- acorns
- seeds and seed pods
- pine cones
- leaves and stems
- pieces of bark

Loose parts presented in an interesting bowl or container make for an engaging provocation.

Sand: The Loosest of Loose Parts

Sand play is quite common in early childhood programs, whether outdoors in playground sandboxes or indoors in sensory tables. Sand is made up of tiny pieces of rocks and minerals, making it the loosest of loose parts. It provides limitless opportunities for creative sensory play.

Sand is also an architectural material. It is used as an aggregate, or a filler and strengthener, in concrete. This means that when children play with sand and water, they are experimenting with some of the same variables engineers use when building concrete structures. Sand will be one of the featured materials in this chapter's projects and activities.

Create Provocations with Natural Materials

Due to the open-ended nature of loose parts, there are endless possibilities for presenting provocations with stones, leaves, shells, and other natural materials. Inspiration can be found in the work of professional artists and architects who work with natural materials. Artist Andy Goldsworthy creates outdoor sculptures using materials such as stones, leaves, and even ice and snow. Images from the book *Andy Goldsworthy: A Collaboration with Nature* (Goldsworthy 1990) may inspire a provocation. For that matter, the images themselves could be presented as provocations.

Architecture books about stonework can also be used for inspiration and provocations. Some examples include *Stone Primer* by Charles McRaven (2007) and *The Spirit of Stone* by Jan Johnson (2017).

You may want to place a provocation in a central, prominent location in the classroom, such as on a main table or rug. You can also present a provocation of loose parts and natural materials in an unexpected place. Perhaps you'll want to arrange a provocation in the block corner. Sticks, stones, and other items from nature are wonderful supplements to a set of wooden unit blocks. The loose parts can be used to decorate block structures and add architectural features such as pathways or porches. You could also place a fan of colorful leaves on an art shelf next to the colored pencils. Or a basket of seed pods could be placed in the book corner next to Dianna Hutts Aston's lovely picture book *A Seed Is Sleepy* (2007).

A provocation of seashells, inspired by the work of Andy Goldsworthy.

DECORATED SANDCASTLES

When it comes to natural materials, one of the most iconic architectural structures we can build is a sandcastle. Any structure made out of wet sand counts as a "castle," even if it doesn't have towers, gables, turrets, parapets, or moats. You can invite children to build any kind of sandcastle or house in a sandbox or on a sensory table.

Sandcastles can be made by mounding and shaping wet, dense sand by hand. A more challenging and engaging form of construction, however, involves buckets, molds, or other containers. First, you pack dense, wet sand into a bucket or mold. Next, you quickly turn the container over and onto the ground or surface. Finally, you gently lift the container so that the sand remains shaped in the form of the container. Once a sand structure is built, children can then use loose parts to embellish and decorate.

Materials

For this activity, sand and water are the main materials. In addition, you will need buckets, molds, or containers as well as a variety of loose parts for decoration (stones, sticks, and so on).

Provocations and Invitations

Sometimes the only nudge children need is a picture of a sandcastle. Engaging picture books about sandcastles and castles in general include the following:

Day at the Beach by Tom Booth (2018)

Sandcastle by Phillip Buntin (2019)

The Sandcastle That Lola Built by Megan Maynor (2018)

Castle by David Macaulay (1982)

Considerations

Adults can support play, exploration, and learning by encouraging children to mix different amounts of water with the sand. The scientific explanation for how wet sand sticks together is based on the concept of surface tension. The water forms a liquid bridge between the grains of sand. So children can see how using different amounts of water affects the texture of the sand and the ability to build a sandcastle that holds together.

Big Ideas and Open-Ended Questions

You can ask questions and make observations that draw children's attention to the texture of the sand and the challenges of building with sand, such as these:

"What do you think makes the sand stick together?"

"Do you need a lot of water or a little water? How can you tell?"

"What happens if the sand is too wet?"

"What happens if the sand is too dry?"

"How can we make this sandcastle stronger?"

"What can we add to this castle to make it more interesting or more beautiful?"

"What happens to the sandcastle when it starts to get dry?"

"What do you think we might do to make our sandcastle last longer?"

Next Steps

If you live in a cold climate, you can use the same techniques to make snow castles or snow forts. After a heavy wet snow, construction can take place on a larger scale. A bucket or mold can be used to make "bricks" that can be stacked to form almost life-size walls. Preschool children will likely need the support and assistance of an adult to coordinate the building of a snow fort, but many will enjoy the challenge. Snow structures can also be colored using diluted watercolor paints or food coloring applied with brushes or spray bottles.

Project 5

TUNNELS AND CANALS

Most young children love digging in sand or dirt, whether with their hands or with tools such as shovels. Why is this? There seems to be a simple yet deep satisfaction gained by digging a hole.

First published in 1952, the picture book *A Hole Is to Dig*, written by Ruth Krauss and illustrated by Maurice Sendak, explores many of the pleasures of digging or discovering holes (Krauss 1989). The childlike text reads, "A hole is when you step in it you go down." It also muses, "Maybe you could hide things in a hole."

With this love of digging, children will enjoy constructing canals and tunnels. These structures serve important purposes in our communities—our homes. The architecture of cities and the design of our built environment rely on canals and tunnels.

Materials

To dig canals and tunnels only two things are needed: something to dig in and something to dig with. Something to dig in could be a sandbox, a patch of dirt, or a sensory table filled with gravel, clay, or other diggable substance. And something to dig with? Some children prefer to dig with their own hands, though many will enjoy using sticks, spoons, or shovels.

Adding water to the process can create excitement, complexity, and challenge. When digging outdoors, children will enjoy access to a water hose or a spigot to fill a bucket. Indoors, offer water in containers, such as small spray bottles or watering cans that the children can pour and manipulate independently.

Provocations and Invitations

In truth, young children don't need provocations or invitations to dig. However, books about canals and tunnels can extend their thinking and challenge them to consider the practical uses of digging. Cutaway illustrations in picture books and nonfiction reference books reveal interesting details about the structure of holes and tunnels.

For example, the picture book *Sam and Dave Dig a Hole*, written by Mac Barnett and illustrated by Jon Klassen (2014), tells the fanciful story of two children digging for treasure. The cutaway illustrations humorously reveal the circuitous route of their tunnel.

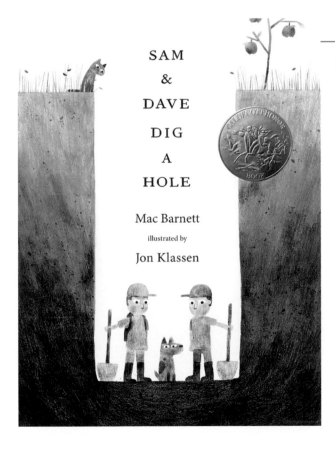

Jon Klassen's illustrations in *Sam and Dave Dig a Hole* show an unusual visual perspective—the cutaway view.

Text copyright © 2014 by Mac Barnett. Illustrations copyright © 2014 by Jon Klassen. Reproduced by permission of the publisher, Candlewick Press, Somerville, MA.

A more realistic picture book, *The Street beneath My Feet* by Charlotte Guillian (2017), reveals the tunnels and other structures built underground in an urban environment through cutaway illustrations. In addition, the nonfiction book *Digging Tunnels* by JoAnn Macken (2008) includes photographs of traffic tunnels and how they were constructed.

Considerations

As children dig, observe their play and listen to their conversations about what they are making. As you engage in conversations with them, look for opportunities to extend and challenge their thinking by introducing ideas from the field of architecture.

Young children may not know the terms *canal* and *tunnel*. You may need to explain and define these words in the context of their play. A canal is a long hole without a roof, usually made to move water from one place to another. A tunnel is a long hole, too, but it usually has a roof. A tunnel can move water, it can be a place for storage, or it can be a passageway for people, cars, and trains.

When digging tunnels, most children will keep digging deeper and deeper until their tunnel collapses. The same is true when children dig canals and try filling them with water. Children will keep digging, hoping their structure will hold the flow of water, only for the sides to collapse and the water to be absorbed into the sand.

These engineering failures are an important part of the learning process; most children don't seem to mind. You can challenge them, though, to think about ways to construct tunnels and canals that are more structurally sound.

A beach is a wonderful setting for sand play for it provides both sand and water.

Big Ideas and Open-Ended Questions

Ask questions and make observations that extend children's ideas about digging holes, canals, and tunnels:

"What kind of hole are you digging?"

"What happens when you dig a very deep hole?"

"What happens when you dig a very long hole?"

"What happens when you put water in a hole?"

"What else can you put inside a hole?"

"What is difficult about making tunnels and canals?"

"How do people make canals and tunnels? What tools and materials do they need?"

Next Steps

Visiting canals or tunnels in your neighborhood can also inspire conversation and exploration. Ideally, find a pedestrian tunnel that children can actually touch and walk through. Also, look for cement culverts that drain water away from roads and bridges—though be sure to teach children to keep a safe distance from these kinds of drainage systems.

Project 6

FAIRY HOUSES

A fairy is a small mythical, magical creature that lives in the woods or other natural areas. Stories about fairies have been told and written for centuries. Tales of the tooth fairy are often shared in American and European families. Among the most classic and enduring stories of fairies are the beautifully illustrated flower fairy stories by Cicely Mary Barker. Another favorite is J. M. Barrie's tale of Peter Pan and the fairy Tinkerbell.

A popular project among gardeners and crafters of all ages is the construction of a fairy house, a tiny structure often built outdoors from natural materials and loose parts. The hope is that a fairy might choose to come and live in it. Many young children enjoy building and working on fairy houses with their parents and teachers, especially when they have recently enjoyed a fairy story.

Building a fairy house is similar in scale to building a dollhouse. In fact, some fairy house architects also make or purchase a fairy figurine to "live" in the house.

Materials

Any of the natural materials and loose parts described in this chapter can be used to build a fairy house. *The Fairy House Handbook* by Liza Gardner Walsh (2012), suggests the following materials:

- pine cones
- bark
- moss
- seaweed
- sticks

- feathers
- shells
- rocks
- acorn caps
- corn silk

- reeds
- pussy willows
- leaves

Provocations and Invitations

A delightful provocation is the shared reading of a favorite fairy story, followed by the invitation to build a house for the fairy in the book. Some suggested picture books that feature fairies or other tiny creatures include the following:

The Complete Book of the Flower Fairies by Cicely Mary Barker (2002)

The Dolls' House Fairy by Jane Ray (2009)

A Fairy Friend by Sue Fliess (2016)

If You See a Fairy Ring by Susanna Lockheart (2007)

Peter in Blueberry Land by Elsa Beskow (1987)

The Little Gardener by Emily Hughes (2018)

Considerations

The first step to constructing a fairy house outdoors is to select an appropriate building site. The house must be built in a quiet spot, where a fairy is most likely to feel safe and welcome. Ask the children to help hunt out a place where a fairy might like to live. Look for natural features that already look like a house, such as the hollow base of a tree or a small "cave" made from leaves and stems.

Next, invite the children to hunt around for natural materials, such as sticks and rocks, that can help define the entrance and other features of the fairy house. A small piece of bark can become a front door, and gravel can be a welcoming walkway. Small objects such as acorn caps can be used as decoration. Children can be encouraged to set up a little fairy picnic, using a leaf as a blanket and shells or seed pods as dishes.

Big Ideas and Open-Ended Questions

As children build and play with their fairy houses, ask questions and make observations that draw their attention to the engineering challenges of building on such a small scale:

"How tall are fairies?"

"What do you think it would be like to be so small?"

"What kind of house do you think a fairy would like to live in?"

"What would such a small fairy use for a bed or for a pillow?"

"What do you think fairies use for food and for dishes?"

"How can we build a house that a fairy would like?"

"What could we do to show the fairy that this is a nice house?"

Next Steps

Invite children to find objects for fairies and fairy houses beyond what can be found in nature. A bottle cap could be a fairy's plate. An ice cream dish could be a fairy's boat. Hunt for these items in your classroom, wash them as needed, and then add them to your creations. (In the next chapter we'll discuss found objects and recyclables.) The goal is to spark conversation as children use their imaginations to think more deeply about life on a small scale.

CHAPTER 3

Found Objects and Recycled Materials

Find a penny,
Pick it up,
And all day long
You'll have good luck!

This age-old rhyme expresses the sense of good fortune we feel when we find something of value in an unexpected place. Perhaps it's a penny on the sidewalk, a beautiful piece of sea glass along the beach, a colorful bottle cap on a playground path. Found objects have magical qualities.

Children seem to feel this thrill of discovery even more strongly than adults. Perhaps this is because the world is so new to young children; nearly every experience is novel and interesting. Or perhaps it's because children feel a sense of power and autonomy when they find something on their own without any adult assistance. If you've ever gone for a walk with a young child or group of young children, you know that they often have a keen eye for spotting interesting items on the ground: a wheel from a broken toy car, an old key that slipped out of someone's pocket long ago, a sticky plastic spoon dropped from a picnic basket.

Items that adults consider trash can be treasure for children. For safety reasons, some items are certainly better left on the ground, or they're better off in a trash can or recycling bin, with an adult's help. But adults can, within reason, support children by helping them make good decisions about which treasures can be saved and used for projects and play.

This chapter describes the wonderful opportunities for invention and construction with found objects and recyclables. This includes small treasures found in unlikely places (such as a bottle cap on the playground) as well as larger materials (such as a milk bottle set aside for recycling).

My preschool students love playing with keys that I have collected over many years of teaching.

Green Architecture

Using found and recycled materials to create construction projects with children very much aligns with the concept of green architecture, an approach to building that minimizes harm to the environment. A "green" building is made from repurposed or sustainable materials, is efficient in its use of energy and water, and/or is built in a way that respects the plants and animals in the immediate environment.

While most preschoolers are too young to study green architecture, they are aware of the importance of being kind to living things. They intuitively understand that construction—whether play or real—should respect people, animals, and plants. Reusing, recycling, and repurposing materials may already be a priority in their families, school, and community. Found materials are also a low-cost way to make the most of your classroom budget.

Cardboard Provocation

Cardboard is a key recyclable for construction play, as you'll discover in the project section that follows. *Caine's Arcade* (2012) is a short documentary film about a little boy who built a huge cardboard game arcade inside his father's used auto parts store in East Los Angeles. The film became a viral sensation on social media and has inspired countless young inventors to create their own cardboard arcade games.

I've frequently used *Caine's Arcade* as a provocation with children of all ages. This film works especially well as a provocation if your school has recently received a shipment of furniture or supplies and a number of cardboard boxes are available for play or construction. When a conversation happens to include the question "What can we make out of cardboard?" it's time to watch *Caine's Arcade*.

Paper towel and toilet paper tubes make wonderful construction materials.

Building with cardboard is not just for children. Architects have been experimenting with cardboard in construction since the 1940s when Buckminster Fuller created a prototype house made of corrugated cardboard. The appeal of cardboard derives from its low cost and environmental sustainability.

Search online for images of cardboard construction, such as the house exhibition at the University of Chongqing in China. Sharing these images can serve as a provocation and inspiration for children's own cardboard inventions.

Project 6

CARDBOARD DOLLHOUSE

Some of my fondest childhood memories involve the cardboard dollhouses I made with my neighborhood friends. We'd find a big box our parents no longer needed. Then we'd draw the squares and rectangles that showed where we wanted the doors and windows to go. We'd try cutting them out ourselves, using our little safety scissors, but usually we'd have to ask a parent or an older sibling to help. A razor box cutter worked best, of course, but only adults were allowed to use that.

I don't remember ever playing with any of our houses; it was the construction and design process we enjoyed the most. We would spend hours adding little details, such as curtains made from tissues or roof shingles made from torn-up brown paper bags.

Creating a house out of a cardboard box is a wonderful activity for home or school. While some adult support may be needed for tricky tasks such as cutting out windows, children can be invited to take the lead in the design and decision-making process. In my experience this project lends itself nicely to a small group of children collaborating on one house.

Materials

The essential building component is a cardboard box the children will turn into a dollhouse. It must be big enough to accommodate the dolls that will be living in it. For instance, a medium-size shipping box is appropriate for dolls or figurines around six to eight inches tall.

In addition, you will need a variety of art supplies for decorating the house, such as paints and scrap paper. Children will also enjoy collecting found objects and recyclables, such as small yogurt cups and jar lids, to use as furniture and household items.

Provocations and Invitations

Interest in creating a dollhouse out of a cardboard box may pop up spontaneously, sparked by ordinary school experiences. Children may spot an empty cardboard box and instantly latch onto the idea of turning it into a house, even without your suggestion. Or you can bring a box into the classroom as a provocation and ask children, "What can we do with this box?"

Reading Giselle Potter's picture book *This Is My Dollhouse* (2016) will likely lead to some interest in creating a cardboard dollhouse. In this story a girl proudly creates her own cardboard dollhouse with features such as hand-drawn wallpaper and an elevator made from a paper cup on a string. She loves her cardboard house—that is, until she goes on a playdate and sees her friend's fancy store-bought dollhouse. Suddenly her handmade house at home doesn't seem quite as nice. Yet both girls soon discover that the best fun is created when you use your imagination and your own hands to create props and stories for your dolls. The illustrations of the girl's creations, such as a dish of spaghetti made from yellow yarn, will surely spark some great ideas for creating a cardboard dollhouse in your classroom.

In the book *This Is My Dollhouse* by Giselle Potter, the main characters discover that a dollhouse they design and build themselves is much more fun than a store-bought dollhouse.

Considerations

Invite the children to participate in the selection of the box and/or the selection of the dolls. This will be a great opportunity to talk about size, measurement, and scale. Have the children hold their doll next to the box and ask, "Do you think this will be a good house for this doll? How big will the door need to be? How tall will the ceilings need to be? Will this doll be comfortable living in a house this size?"

As children work on their house, be ready to assist with a few steps. As mentioned above, cutting out the doors and windows requires a box cutter or sharp scissors. This task should only be done by adults, but the children can create the lines that map out the placement of these features. Another alternative is not to cut the cardboard at all and let the children draw the details and use their imaginations to fill in the rest.

When preschool children work together on a collaborative task such as building a cardboard dollhouse, they will inevitably have questions and conflicts. Who gets to decide how the house will be designed? Who gets to decorate it? Who gets to play with it?

These issues are wonderful opportunities to model a process for collaborative decision-making, which involves listening to one another's ideas and taking turns. Remember that young children are just starting to learn to use these social skills. They will often need an adult to facilitate and help resolve issues that come up.

Keep in mind, too, that making a cardboard dollhouse is not a quick and easy project. The initial setup—positioning the house, cutting off the lid or side for easy access to the inside, adding the doors and windows—may take several sessions. Adding features and furniture can take place over weeks or even months. Don't be concerned if the children's interest in playing with the dollhouse wanes after they have finished making it. Again, the pleasure is in the process.

Big Ideas and Open-Ended Questions

As children work, ask questions and make observations that draw their attention to the architectural features of the dollhouse as well as the design elements involved in building a real house.

"What are the parts of a house?"

"What makes a house sturdy and safe?"

"How will the dolls go in and out of this house?"

"How will they get from the first floor to the second floor?"

"What will the dolls do inside this house?

"What rooms do they need? What kinds of furniture will they need?"

"What will happen when it rains or the weather gets cold? Will this house keep the dolls warm and dry?"

Next Steps

Children may be surprised and delighted to learn that making doll-sized houses and furniture are activities that adults enjoy as much as children. Making a dollhouse is part of a large tradition among hobbyists and artists who love to make miniatures, which are items and environments made on a small scale. This includes everything from tiny dioramas carved into walnut shells to huge model-train cities. With your help, children can explore how adults have taken on these activities.

For example, *The Mouse Mansion* by Dutch artist Karina Schaapman (2014) is an amazing picture book containing photographs of an elaborately crafted miniature house she made from cardboard and papier-mâché. Children will enjoy studying the photos to discover the various materials (often found objects) that were used to create the mouse's home. Another great example of a beautifully detailed miniature environment is Colleen Moore's *Fairy Castle* at the Museum of Science and Industry in Chicago.

Of course, creating an entire house is not necessary for children to enjoy making miniatures. Anytime children build on a small scale, whether they are molding a tiny chair out of clay or padding a little box with cotton to make a doll's bed, they are gaining experience with design engineering and practicing important STEM skills.

Project 8

FABRIC TENTS AND FORTS

A tent is shelter made of cloth, supported by poles or a frame. Usually a tent is a temporary structure, providing shade during a visit to the beach or a place to sleep on a camping trip.

Many children enjoy constructing their own makeshift tents out of sheets, blankets, chairs—anything available in the present moment. With a little make-believe, a tent may become a fort, which children can imagine themselves defending from outside forces. The common couch fort, made by propping up cushions and draping a sheet across the top to form a roof, is a classic example of repurposing found materials. (In this case, materials that will have to be returned to their proper places after the fun is over.)

Most preschools don't have a collection of couch cushions and living room furniture available, but with a little gentle facilitation, children can still design and build fabric constructions at school.

Materials

A large, lightweight bedsheet works best. A fitted sheet may seem a poor choice at first because the elastic hem will keep the sheet from lying flat. However, the elastic hem may actually help the sheet stay in place when stretched between several chairs or other pieces of furniture.

Blankets are heavier than sheets. They present an added engineering challenge.

Chairs and small tables can be used to prop up the fabric to form the roof. Providing clothespins, binder clips, and rope or string will add further design and construction options. Other optional materials include scarves, umbrellas, and Hula-Hoops.

Provocations and Invitations

A single sheet draped over a small table creates not only an inviting shelter but also a provocation for further exploration of the concept of tents. Invite children to crawl under the table and enter the little table-tent. Ask the children open-ended questions that explore their ideas and sense of curiosity around the topics of tents, forts, shelter, and hiding. Ask, "What do you like about this little tent? How could we make it bigger? How do you think we could make it better?"

Another idea is to present the children with a sheet and ask, "How can we use this to make a tent? What else do we need? How will we build it?"

Considerations

Support and facilitate the children's ideas with whatever materials and space you have available. Encourage them to think creatively. Perhaps one side of the sheet could be secured to a windowsill with binder clips and the other side draped over several chairs.

Anticipate that problems may arise in construction, but let the children take the lead in fixing them. For example, if the sheet keeps sliding off the back of a round chair, you might say, "I see how the sheet keeps slipping here. How can we secure it?" Show the children some options, such as tape or clips, and see which one they would like to try.

And at some point the roof of the tent will likely cave in. This happens as children play inside the tent, causing the roof or sides to get jostled and moved. This is another valuable teachable moment. You can facilitate a troubleshooting conversation in which the children identify what might be causing the problem, brainstorm possible solutions, and then select a promising strategy to try out.

Big Ideas and Open-Ended Questions

As children build and play inside their tent, ask questions and make observations that help draw their attention to the architectural features and design elements of tent structures.

"How is a tent different from a regular house?"

"What do you like about being inside a tent? How does it feel to be in it?"

"What do you see when you're inside a tent? Is it dark? Why is it dark in a tent?"

"How will you go in and out of your tent? Do you need a door?"

Next Steps

For aspiring young architects who are fascinated by unusual construction techniques for shelters, introduce them to geodesic domes. A geodesic dome is a round, lightweight structure made of many parts that form triangles and other shapes. Like the design of a traditional tent, a geodesic dome has a supporting frame and an outer covering—what architects call the "skin" of a building.

Many playgrounds have a round climbing structure that is shaped like a geodesic dome. As you explore the dome together, ask open-ended questions, such as, "How is this like the tent we made in class? How is it different?" and "What would you need to build or add to this structure to make it more like a tent or a house?"

For older preschoolers and kindergarteners, you can also encourage them to build a scaled-down geodesic dome out of recycled or repurposed materials, such as rolled-up newspaper or straws. You can find many helpful guides and videos online. It's a challenging activity that will likely require the support of a teacher or parent, but it may be well worth the effort.

Many school and public playgrounds include a coverless geodesic dome as a climbing structure.

RECYCLED PLASTIC NEIGHBORHOOD

What's in your recycling bin right now? Chances are you have many plastic bottles and food containers. Those plastic items can be repurposed as construction materials for creative children.

The variety of shapes and sizes of plastic recyclables naturally lends itself to designing a miniature urban landscape. Place a large piece of paper or cardboard on a tabletop, and then invite the children to help you map out a grid of streets and intersections. Once the neighborhood is plotted, encourage children to turn the recyclables—with the help of tape and decorations—into homes, stores, and other buildings to place on the streets.

Materials

For this activity you'll need to collect a wide variety of clean plastic containers. Some prep work may be required for the collection and cleaning of the containers.

You'll also need something the children can use to make the containers stick together. Adhering plastic to plastic is difficult because the surface is so smooth. Masking tape works well, but young children often have trouble peeling the tape from the roll. For this reason you'll want to use masking tape that's in a dispenser or provide a supply of precut pieces of tape gently adhered to the edge of a table. You may need to demonstrate how the masking tape can be used to attach two plastic items together.

A large piece of paper or cardboard works well as your neighborhood grid. You'll need markers to draw out the streets. In addition, you may want to provide construction paper scraps, stickers, and other collage materials to decorate the containers or add architectural features such as doors and windows.

Provocations and Invitations

A simple provocation is to gather the plastic recyclables and place them on an activity table along with the tape. Invite children to build by asking, "What can you make with these plastic containers? Do any of these shapes remind you of houses? Do you think we could build houses for a neighborhood?"

Another idea is to place the recyclables in the block corner. Children innately equate the block corner with building, construction, and architecture. Seeing novel materials in a familiar place may lead to exciting ideas. Have some masking tape pieces prepped and ready in case children express an interest in attaching recyclables together. They may also be inspired to incorporate recyclables into their block structures in innovative combinations.

Considerations

Children may instantly take to building with recyclables, or they may need a little help and scaffolding to reimagine and repurpose the materials. The easiest technique for building with plastic containers is simple stacking. Yogurt tubs with lids work especially well for stacking into towers.

Alternatively, each container could be an individual building. Nudging children to decorate the containers as homes may help make the transformation more complete. Ask children, "If this were a little house, where would you put the door? Where would you put the windows?" Provide markers, tape, and construction paper as needed.

Big Ideas and Open-Ended Questions

As children think about how they can make homes and a neighborhood out of plastic containers, some will benefit from questions and suggestions to spark ideas, such as these:

"Can you make a house out of plastic? How would you do that?"

"How would you make the walls? How would you make a roof?"

"What does this plastic container look like to you? Does it look like a building or a part of a building?"

"If you lived in this house, what would your neighborhood look like? What would your street look like? Who might live nearby?"

"How can you turn these plastic houses into a neighborhood? Which buildings belong together? What else do you need to make a neighborhood?"

Next Steps

Most plastic containers, such as water bottles, are cylindrical. The rounded sides of these containers create an engineering challenge. It is difficult to stack them like blocks.

Therefore, some young architects may appreciate the opportunity to incorporate cardboard in the creation of their plastic recyclable construction projects. For example, water bottles or yogurt containers can serve as pillars between "floors" of flat cardboard. Using mixed materials opens up new levels (sometimes literally) of design possibilities.

CHAPTER 4

Wood

Most of us are familiar with wood. Archaeological evidence of people building with wood dates back as far as ten thousand years. Wood still remains a popular choice today, and it is especially valued as an environmentally friendly and renewable resource. You probably have wooden furniture at home or at work. You might be sitting on wood right now. Many of our houses and schools are at least partly made out of wood.

Children begin to understand at an early age that wood comes from trees and that it's an important building material. They recognize that real things are made out of wood. Things that we use every day. Things that last a long time.

As mentioned in chapter 1, wood is an ideal material for unit blocks. Wooden unit blocks are light enough for a child to lift but not too light to build with. The natural color and smooth texture of sanded wood make block construction a pleasure.

Moving beyond unit blocks, wood is a great material for other forms of construction and architectural play. Lincoln Logs have been childhood staples for more than a hundred years, and KEVA planks are also popular today. For an even more natural approach, sticks can be collected from outside for construction projects.

Of the three projects in this chapter, two are basic building activities involving wooden construction toys and scrap pieces. The third project, however, takes us a step further. It introduces tools as an important part of woodworking and carpentry.

Wood is well suited for all kinds of construction and architectural play.

Simple carpentry projects expose children to an even deeper enjoyment of wood. Teaching children to work with wood can be a satisfying, empowering experience for both teachers and children. Children feel respected and valued when given an opportunity to use real tools, such as hammers, hand drills, and screwdrivers. Even those of us with limited woodworking experience are probably familiar with the smell of freshly sanded wood. When we saw and sand wood, or drive nails or screws into wood, we enjoy an even richer sensory experience of sounds, sights, and smells.

However, working with wood and using authentic tools can be dangerous if not done properly. A sense of risk is involved, which many children find exciting and many teachers and parents find terrifying. Establishing and following clear safety guidelines is an important part of the process, as we will discuss later in the chapter.

Twenty-First-Century Woodworking

For ages, it seems, woodworking was viewed as a craft only certain people could master or even explore. For example, woodworking books and magazines published in the midtwentieth century typically include photos of suburban men in plaid shirts, building bookshelves in their basements. In recent years

With a little bit of research and practice, any early childhood educator can be successful at facilitating woodworking projects.

woodworking has made its way into many new areas, including early childhood education.

This cultural shift is part of the maker movement. One of the core ideas behind the movement is the inclusive idea that we are all makers (Dougherty 2012). People of all ages and abilities, genders and cultures, can and should be encouraged to learn to build, invent, design, and create, including with wood. In 2005 *Make* magazine was founded, and there is a worldwide network of Maker Faires.

Although the maker movement originally involved adult hobbyists, many schools and classrooms have created "makerspaces" as well. These are work-spaces where children can learn how to use authentic tools and design and engineer whatever their creativity inspires them to make—learning valuable STEM skills along the way. Introducing even young children to woodworking is a great way to capture the spirit of this movement.

In his article "Irresistible Learning: Woodwork in Early Childhood Education," early childhood educator Pete Moorhouse (2018a) notes another important reason for twenty-first-century learners to acquire woodworking skills. He proposes that woodworking provides important relief from screen time and children's increasing engagement with digital devices. Moorhouse writes, "Woodwork can be seen as a wonderful alternative [to digital activities], engaging children with real tools and authentic materials. Woodwork also provides children with an experience of making and repairing as opposed to our prevailing culture of consuming and disposing."

Introducing Woodworking to Children

A helpful first resource for talking with children about the importance of wood is Gail Gibbons's (1990) classic picture book *How a House Is Built.* The illustrations demonstrate a step-by-step process for creating a wood frame house.

Additionally, you may wish to visit an actual building site where a wood frame structure is under construction. It can serve as an inspiring destination for a field trip or neighborhood walk. Children will begin to see how their wood projects in the classroom relate to real-life projects in the built environment.

To pave the way for carpentry projects, you'll also need to introduce tools. In particular, I like using Montessori bolt boards as a safe and accessible way to take those first steps. These smooth wooden boards come with a carved slot that holds a tool—a wrench or a screwdriver—next to a row of base screws of various sizes. The screws are securely attached to the board, along with the corresponding bolts or screws the child can manipulate with the tool.

Although I am not trained as a Montessori educator, I value the bolt board and many of the other teaching materials used in Montessori classrooms. And although these materials were created as part of the Practical Life curriculum in a Montessori classroom, they can also be used in non-Montessori classrooms as a manipulative or as a prop in pretend play.

Another step in preparing for woodworking with children is an investment in a child-sized workbench. Securing a piece of wood in a clamp or vise at the appropriate height is very important for ensuring children's safety when sawing or drilling. Another essential but less expensive piece of equipment is safety goggles or glasses. Both adults and children should protect their eyes with safety goggles or glasses whenever they are working with wood and tools.

And of course, you can't introduce woodworking without wood itself. The first time I developed a woodworking curriculum, I sought out donations of wood scraps from home improvement stores and local woodshops. I was surprised to discover, however, that many of the scraps were unsuitable because the wood was too hard. The children struggled to apply enough force to pound nails or drill holes in even our simplest carpentry projects.

For this reason I've found that sometimes it's necessary to purchase very soft wood for the children's first experiences rather than use donated scraps. For example, maple and cherry are quite hard, while pine and cedar are much softer.

Once the children learn how to use the tools safely, the classroom woodworking area can be used throughout the day.

Safety First

Safety must come first if you choose to teach preschool children to use real woodworking tools. This is one of the rare times when direct instruction is necessary and appropriate. Orientation to a new tool should be done one-on-one, not in groups, and under close adult supervision. You may need extra teachers or volunteers to provide the one-on-one supervision necessary.

It's important for all the adults—teachers as well as volunteers—to know up front which children will require the most assistance. I've also found it helpful to develop a tool checklist to mark which children have learned to appropriately use each type of tool.

Another essential step in ensuring safety is making sure that no sharp objects, such as tools and nails, are left unattended in the classroom. Be sure to sweep the floor and check the area thoroughly after cleanup.

LOG CABIN

Lincoln Logs were a wildly popular toy in the 1950s and 1960s and are still available today. These interlocking notched wooden logs fit together at right angles in alternating patterns, making them perfect to form the walls and frame of a log cabin.

These construction toys have an interesting history. They were invented by John Lloyd Wright, the son of the famous American architect Frank Lloyd Wright. John was inspired to invent Lincoln Logs after he joined his father on a trip to Tokyo to oversee the construction of his father's design for the Imperial Hotel.

The hotel was built with the floating cantilever construction technique. This helped protect the building from earthquake damage. The overlapping and interlocking beams in this building inspired John to invent Lincoln Logs. As the primary material in the toy, he chose wood, which he called "the most humanly intimate of all materials" (Sweet n.d.). Sets were sold to families starting in 1918.

Materials

Building a log cabin with Lincoln Logs does not require any special woodworking tools. All you need is a set of Lincoln Logs.

Lincoln Logs are shaped to fit together as interlocking beams.

Otherwise, you can use thick straight sticks that are fairly uniform in size and length. (About eight to ten inches long is ideal.) You'll probably need at least twenty-four sticks to create a nice cabin frame. If collecting sticks with children, find one ideal stick and ask the children to help you find other sticks that match it. Before play, remove any leaves or stems from the sticks, and trim off any sharp ends. You can also involve the children in this process.

Plank blocks such as KEVA also work well. You may even wish to use pieces from another classic toy: Jenga. To play Jenga you first build a tower of fifty-four wooden blocks in alternating layers, not unlike the overlapping beams of Lincoln Logs. You then take turns removing one block at a time until the tower collapses. Most preschool children do not yet have the dexterity and small motor skills to play a game of Jenga, but they can use the blocks for making "log cabins" with the alternating building technique.

Provocations and Invitations

As a provocation prepare a section of a wall or fence demonstrating the overlapping, alternating technique. Place the structure, along with the Lincoln Logs, in a prominent place. The idea here is to show the children how the pieces fit together so they can begin to understand how to use these materials. Invite children to build their own structure by imitating the same technique or inventing their own methods of construction.

This cabin was constructed using techniques similar to the way children build with Lincoln Logs.

Images of real log cabins can also serve as a provocation or inspiration. A search online can provide log cabin photos and even building plans. If possible, look for creative cabins that stretch the imagination beyond just a simple four-wall square building.

You may also wish to share architectural books about log cabins. Two examples are *Cabins: A Guide to Building Your Own Nature Retreat* by David and Jeanie Stiles (2001) and *The Family Cabin: Inspiration for Camps, Cottages, and Cabins* by Dale Mulfinger (2017).

Considerations

Some children will take right to this activity, eager to build log cabins with the alternating pattern. Other children, though, might be new to Lincoln Logs, or they might need help with the alternating technique. A little guidance and demonstration will get them moving in the right direction.

If needed, have children first practice the alternating pattern using plank blocks or even ordinary sticks, which might be easier to work with. Once they're familiar with the building technique, invite them to try to execute it using Lincoln Logs. Help them discover how lining up the notches allows the logs to lock together.

Big Ideas and Open-Ended Questions

As children practice stacking the logs in an alternating pattern, ask questions and make observations that draw their attention to the engineering challenges involved with building a log cabin, such as these:

"How is building with logs different from building with blocks and bricks?"

"How might you make a roof and a door for your cabin?"

"How might you make a window?"

"How big will your cabin be?"

"Who lives in this cabin? Where will they sleep and eat?"

"Some people build real houses out of logs. How do you think they do it? What do you think they do to make sure the logs fit together and stay together?"

Next Steps

As children work on their log cabins, they may notice that this building technique leaves gaps between the logs. In real architecture a gap between logs is called a chink, and the material used to fill the gap is also called chink.

Ask children, "What can we do about that gap? How could we make the log cabin stronger?" Some children may become interested in using clay or playdough "chink" to fill the gaps.

Project 11

THE "SLAPDASH" HOUSE

The expression "slapdash" means doing something quickly and, perhaps, carelessly. Here we're using the term to describe a wood house constructed with glue and decorated with paint. In other words, the "slap" is the glue and the "dash" is the paint.

This activity is intended for children who are eager to start working with wood but may not yet have experience with (or access to) hammers, nails, and other tools. An interest in building with wood often arises through ordinary block play. When children work hard on a block structure and they are pleased with the results, it's natural that they would want to keep what they made (especially at cleanup time!). When these conversations happen, you can offer this activity as a way to build something more permanent out of wood scraps. Many children will be thrilled by this suggestion and will look forward to the opportunity.

Materials

The most important material for this project is a collection of scrap wood pieces of various shapes and sizes. Be sure to sand any rough edges to prevent splinters.

Depending on the number of wood scraps you have available, you may want to establish guidelines about how many pieces of wood each child will be allowed to use in their creation. A selection of four to six pieces per child works well.

You will also need wood glue or regular white glue (school glue). Wood glue will form a strong bond, but it is not washable and could stain clothing. If you use wood glue, be sure to have children wear smocks. Regular white glue will be fine for working with small, light pieces of wood.

For the decoration phase, you'll want to provide tempera or acrylic paint and brushes. Again, children should wear smocks if the paint is not washable.

Provocations and Invitations

As a warm-up activity, provide a variety of wood scraps in the block area and encourage open-ended play. Let the children know that they will soon have the opportunity to make their own permanent structure out of these wood scraps, but for now they are just trying out different ways of putting things together. This type of preview construction practice and play—before glue and paint are involved—will allow children to be more intentional and successful with their slapdash houses.

Considerations

Some children may want to build houses and buildings, while others may choose to build free-form structures and works of art. The wide variety is a natural outcome when working with a mix of wood scraps and a mix of creative minds.

Keep in mind that this is not a quick project. The process of gluing wood and letting it dry may take several days. Some of the glued pieces may need to be secured with a clamp or tape while the glue dries. These challenges are wonderful learning experiences for the children and may involve trial and error.

When the creations are completely assembled, all the pieces in place, and the glue dry, only then can the painting begin. Adding paint to a finished wood structure is like adding the frosting to a cake!

Big Ideas and Open-Ended Questions

As children assemble and glue their structures, ask questions such as the following that draw their attention to the characteristics of wood as well as to the shapes and sizes of the wood scraps:

"Tell me about what you are making. How did you decide what to make?"

"Which wood pieces did you pick? Why did you pick them?"

"What do you like about building with wood?"

Next Steps

Through this project children will observe and learn that gluing is not the strongest way to put wood together. This experience will likely lead to an interest in using real tools, such as a hammer and nails, to put wood together.

HOLES AS HOMES

Tiny things live in tiny homes. This is true in nature as well as in the world of make-believe. Tiny ants live in tiny tunnels dug into sand and soil. Little owls live in hollows of trees. The fictional Borrowers, tiny people featured in the book series by Mary Norton, live in the small spaces under the floorboards of a "big people" house.

An exploration of the idea of holes as homes can lead in many different directions, including opportunities to practice using authentic woodworking tools. Here children will be introduced to a rotary hand drill.

Teaching children how to use a real drill to make holes in wood may sound like a difficult and dangerous task. That's because most of us are only familiar with power drills. But children as young as three years old can safely manage a manual rotary hand drill, with proper supervision.

Materials

A manual rotary hand drill is sometimes called an "eggbeater" drill. It operates not unlike an eggbeater, where you turn a crank to move a twist bit at the end.

You will also need a large piece of scrap wood. As mentioned earlier, soft varieties of wood will be best. To prepare your drilling surface, secure the wood to a workbench.

As a simple alternative, you may wish to have children drill directly into a tree stump outdoors or into a wood "cookie" indoors. A cookie is a cross section slice of a tree. It should be heavy, thick, and secure.

Provocations and Invitations

Sharing a story might be a great way to inspire an exploration of holes as homes. *Cat & Mouse* by Britta Tekentrup (2019) is just one example of a lovely picture book that features an animal or other small character that lives in a hole in a wall or tree. Other books include *Owl Babies* by Martin Wadell (2002) and *Frederick* by Leo Lionni (1967).

You may wish to ask children to share their own firsthand knowledge of creatures living in little holes, such as the ants that live in hills found in the cracks in the sidewalk. Invite the children to go on a "hole hunt" indoors or outdoors, looking for little spaces where tiny creatures, real or imagined, might live.

You can also inspire children with an open invitation to create holes of all kinds, using materials and items you may already have available. For example, you could encourage children to dig holes in sand using spoons or shovels, or to poke holes in paper or foam using pencils or knitting needles. These will be good warm-up activities prior to working with wood and a hand drill.

Considerations

As emphasized throughout the chapter, safety comes first when working with real tools. Teach children that anyone working with wood should begin by wearing protective eye gear. Next, demonstrate one-on-one how to use the drill, taking care to show children where to place their hands, balance the drill, and turn the handle.

You may wish to create pilot holes by predrilling small shallow holes in the wood prior to the activity. This will give beginning drillers a spot to rest the bit and balance the drill before they turn the handle.

Big Ideas and Open-Ended Questions

While children are using the drill, it's important that they stay focused on the task. But once children are done, or as they observe other children using the drill, ask questions that draw their attention to how the tool works and the ways it changes the wood:

"Which parts of the drill stay still? Which parts move?"

"What is difficult or scary about using a drill?"

"What is fun and easy about using a drill?"

"What happens to the wood when the drill bit moves and turns?"

"Does the wood look different now? Does it smell different now?"

"What do you like about working with wood?"

"What kind of hole have you made?"

"Could this hole be a home? Why or why not?"

Next Steps

Discussions of holes as homes may lead to an interest in the concept of caves and the animals that live in them. The classic picture book *We're Going on a Bear Hunt* by Michael Rosen and illustrated by Helen Oxenbury (2003) features a family finding a bear in a cave. Nonfiction resources, such as *All about Bears* by Jennifer Syzmanski (2019), can provide accurate information about bear habitats. Children may enjoy digging small caves for toy animals in a sandbox or dirt pile.

Using a hand drill can lead to an interest in using other tools, such as hammers, screwdrivers, and saws. In my experience working with young children, the tool they most covet is the hammer. Most preschool children have seen someone use a hammer, and they usually understand its purpose and function. Everyone—children, especially—seem to enjoy hitting things with a hammer. The key is making sure children learn to use a hammer and other tools safely.

And of course, these simple forays into woodworking may inspire children to take on more-challenging projects. Remember, though, that young children will need to regularly practice developing skills to build a box or a birdhouse. For guidance, I recommend Patsy Skeen's and Anita Garner's (1984) classic *Woodworking for Young Children* or Pete Moorhouse's (2018b) *Learning through Woodwork*.

Working, playing, and building with wood is a wonderful outdoor activity.

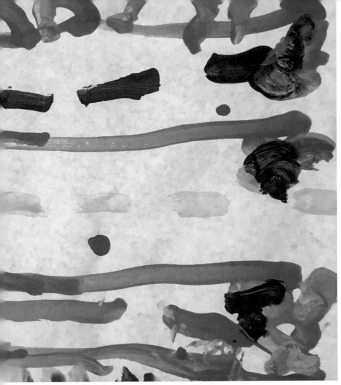

PART 2
Explorations

CHAPTER 5

Architecture Stories

Beautifully illustrated picture books inspire children—and adults as well—to see the world through new eyes. This is especially true when the book is about architecture, construction, and buildings. Reading aloud to children and sharing beautifully illustrated stories is an essential component in developing children's creativity and their interest in architecture. Once you look at children's picture books through the lens of architecture, you will find inspiration everywhere.

Let's begin with classic picture books. From the teetering towering home of the Once-ler in the opening of Dr. Seuss's (1971) *The Lorax* to the city of windows in Crockett Johnson's (1955) *Harold and the Purple Crayon*, classic children's books contain a fascinating variety of architectural structures.

One of the most expansive examples of architecture in a classic children's book is Richard Scarry's detailed illustrations of Busytown, as featured in several books, including *What Do People Do All Day?* (2015), *Best Word Book Ever* (1999), and *Cars and Trucks and Things That Go* (1998). Students of architecture will recognize that the Busytown town hall and the auto shop are built in a distinctively late Tudor style, as demonstrated by the pattern of dark beams over light plaster. The Busytown dentist's office is located in a building with a clay tile roof in a Spanish Mission style. But not all the Busytown structures are built in a traditional style of architecture. Interestingly and aptly, the shoe repair shop is in a building shaped like a shoe!

From Busytown and beyond, children's books can inspire early education construction projects. Let's explore how architecture stories can come to life in your classroom.

The illustrations in Richard Scarry's classic picture books contain a wide variety of architecturally interesting buildings.

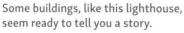

Some buildings, like this lighthouse, seem ready to tell you a story.

Novel Engineering

Developed by the University Center for Engineering Education Outreach at Tufts University, novel engineering is a literacy-based approach to teaching engineering-related STEM skills. With this approach educators use texts, such as children's literature, as the inspiration for engineering projects. For example, elementary school students reading *The Wizard of Oz* might create a project in which they build a yellow brick road leading to Emerald City. This type of integrated learning deepens their understanding of the text while at the same time developing STEM skills related to engineering.

In early childhood, read-aloud picture books can provide inspiration for novel engineering projects. In particular, picture books can inspire projects related to houses and architecture. For example, the well-known story of the three little pigs and the big bad wolf provides several opportunities (three, to be exact) for children to take the story off the page and create an engineering project. Children can build models of the straw house, the stick house, and the brick house. They can then use a fan or blow dryer to represent the huffing and puffing of the big bad wolf to test and compare the resilience of the three houses.

Provocations

Whether you call it "novel engineering" or "picture book provocations," children's literature often inspires creative ideas and explorations related to architecture. A few rare and wonderful children's picture books are explicitly about architecture and architects. These include the following:

Iggy Peck, Architect by Andrea Beaty (2007)

How a House Is Built by Gail Gibbons (1990)

If I Built a House by Chris Van Dusen (2012)

Billions of Bricks by Kurt Cyrus (2016)

Building a House by Byron Barton (1990)

Windows by Julia Denos (2017)

Picture books can also lead to construction projects even when the story itself isn't about architecture. One of my favorite examples is Mo Willem's (2004) picture book *Knuffle Bunny*. The illustrations are an ingenious mix of realistic black-and-white background photos with main characters drawn in Willem's characteristic animated style. The photos depict a friendly urban landscape—the sidewalk and front stoops of the Park Slope neighborhood in Brooklyn.

The story of Knuffle Bunny is not about architecture but of a lost toy that is accidently left behind at the Laundromat. The photos in the book allow us to easily imagine the setting of the story, which centers on two distinct locations: the home where the little girl, Trixie, lives with her family and the Laundromat where Trixie and her daddy wash their clothes. The text gives specific directions for traveling between the two locations: "down the block, through the park, past the school."

With its delightfully relatable story, *Knuffle Bunny* lends itself very well to a little novel engineering. Many children will be inspired to build Trixie's Park Slope neighborhood out of blocks, including representations of Trixie's house, the sidewalk, the park, the school, and (of course) the Laundromat. It's just one example of how a seemingly simple picture book can invite children to explore the world of architecture and our built environment.

The Architecture of Books

The physical structure of a book has its own architecture—the construction of the spine, the binding, the cover, and the pages. This itself is something to explore with children, comparing and contrasting a book's construction to a building's.

In addition, pop-up and lift-the-flap books have special interactive details that demonstrate creative paper engineering. Other books have transparent overlays that bring us under the surface of the book and its contents. Some of these special books are specifically about architectural concepts, such as the following:

Pop-up Books

The Architecture Pop-Up Book by Anton Radevsky (2009)

Castle: Medieval Days and Knights by Kyle Olmon (2006)

Pop-Up New York by Andy Mansfield (2016)

Popville by Anouck Boisrobert and Louis Rigaud (2010)

Lift-the-Flap Books

All Kinds of Homes by Emma Damon (2005)

Open House by Steve Noon (1996)

See Inside Houses Long Ago by Rob Jones (2010)

Transparent Overlay Books

Magic Colors by Patrick George (2013)

Castles by Gallemard Jeunesse et al. (1993)

Dinosaurs by Gallemard Jeunesse (1993)

The Rain Forest by Gallemard Jeunesse (1994)

The Egg by Rene Mettler (2012)

VIRGINIA LEE BURTON'S LITTLE HOUSE

The Little House, written and illustrated by Virginia Lee Burton (1978), was first published in 1942, but it is still in print and well loved today. The story follows a new house built out in the country. Over the passage of many years, the little house watches how the land around it is built up with roads and buildings. Eventually the little house is completely surrounded by subways and high-rises. The story ends happily when the great-great-granddaughter of the original owners recognizes the house and moves it to a new location, out in a remote rural area, similar to the place she was first built.

The Little House is an unusual book in many ways. The main character is a house that does not speak or act; it simply watches the world around itself. The story chronicles the advancement of technology and urban sprawl over the course of four decades. The elegant, simple text and the beautifully designed illustrations demonstrate the passage of time in ways that even young children can understand.

The Little House lends itself very well to novel engineering. Reading it aloud to children is sure to spark many interesting conversations and open-ended explorations. Creating a model of the little house is one project that can grow from the story, but the illustrations and text present many additional engineering challenges: roads, other buildings, transportation systems, and more.

Materials

This is an open-ended project, which means there is no one way to approach it. Construction projects inspired by *The Little House* can be built with any of the materials described in this book, including blocks and LEGO bricks, found items, recyclables, and wood. Depending on the materials and the direction the children take the project, you may also wish to provide art supplies for decoration.

Provocations and Invitations

In addition to reading *The Little House*, you may wish to take the class for a walk. Children may be inspired by the houses and buildings in their own neighborhood or the area around their school. If possible, look for structures represented in the illustrations, such as paved roads, streetlights, apartment buildings, and elevated trains.

Combining colored blocks with unit blocks helps this little block house wear a friendly face.

After hearing the story, some children will be particularly curious about the idea of moving a whole house from one location to another. Search online for real-life images of houses being moved on trucks. These images will no doubt inspire someone to build a house on a toy truck or other wheeled toy.

Considerations

Children will naturally gravitate toward building little houses of their own. With a little prompting, you can nudge them toward constructing a built environment all around it that includes the following:

- Roads: Ask children, "In the story, how were the roads made? What kinds of equipment and materials were used to make the roads?" Suggest that children try to make similar roads in the sandbox, sensory table, or outdoors in the soil or grass.

- Other buildings: Ask children, "What other types of buildings were built? How were they made? Were they bigger or smaller than the little house? How do you know?" Suggest that children try building other structures near the little house, just as the buildings were added in the story.

- Trolleys, trains, and subways: Invite the children to study the illustrations of the trolleys, elevated trains, and subways. Suggest that children try building subways and roads as well.

- Lighting: In the story the little house notices the difference between the light from the moon and the stars and the light from the streetlamps and buildings. Invite children to use flashlights, battery-powered tea lights, string lights, and/or LED lights to their construction projects to create different lighting effects.

Big Ideas and Open-Ended Questions

As children work on construction projects inspired by *The Little House*, ask questions and make observations that will draw their attention to the architectural elements and engineering concepts demonstrated in the story.

"What are the parts and features of the little house? How many windows does it have? What kind of roof does it have?"

"What do you think the inside of the little house looks like? How many rooms do you think it has? What types of rooms?"

"Who might live in a house like this? What might they do here? What kinds of furniture would they need?"

"If you made a storybook about this house, how would it begin? What else might happen?"

Next Steps

Virginia Lee Burton's story gives the little house a personality and perspective. We care about the little house and what happens to it as if it were a person. The story may spark some conversations among the children about whether a house can be alive and have feelings. Invite the children to create their own stories about the buildings they know.

Project 14

BIRD'S-EYE VIEW

When children build with blocks on the floor and then stand above their work, looking down at what they made, they are able to see their structures as if from a bird's-eye view. This is a perspective rarely seen when looking at real, life-size buildings. It is a wonderful opportunity for children to reflect on the characteristics of their buildings—their shape, their size, their relation to other buildings. A view from above is also similar to the perspective needed to create a map or blueprint, a topic we'll address in the next chapter.

Yellow Umbrella, written by Dong Il Sheen (2002), is a wordless picture book that beautifully demonstrates a bird's-eye view. The illustrations by Jae-Soo Liu show the progress of a child carrying a yellow umbrella on her walk to school. They are painted from a perspective that looks down from the clouds. A lovely soundtrack featuring both music and acoustic effects can be played to accompany the "reading" of the illustrations.

To help bring the story to life, children can be invited to incorporate small paper umbrellas, the kind used to decorate tropical cocktails, into their construction projects. Whether children build houses, skyscrapers, or other buildings, the umbrellas can be a reminder for them to observe their projects from a bird's-eye view.

Provocations and Invitations

Yellow Umbrella is a wonderful provocation by itself. After sharing it with the class, you can draw their attention to an array of paper umbrellas waiting in the block corner or on an activity table.

When viewed from above, the little paper umbrellas look like the illustrations from the book *Yellow Umbrella*.

Materials

As this is another open-ended project, children may build with blocks and LEGO bricks, found items, recyclables, wood, or other construction materials. Children may wish to add toy figures to their buildings.

In addition, you can supply small paper cocktail umbrellas (available from kitchen or party supply stores). You may need to open the umbrellas for children in advance; they can be quite fragile. You may also want to provide small amounts of clay to hold the umbrellas for placement on the construction projects.

Considerations

Because *Yellow Umbrella* is a wordless picture book, invite children to talk about what they see while you are viewing the illustrations. Some children may not initially understand the perspective of the pictures. Ask open-ended questions, such as, "What do you see?" and "What do you think is happening here?" When a child makes an observation such as, "They're walking down some stairs," invite the child to explain their thinking by asking, "How do you know?" Children may benefit from multiple viewings of the picture book on several different occasions, as they are likely to notice something new each time.

Big Ideas and Open-Ended Questions

As children incorporate the paper umbrellas into their construction play, ask questions and make observations that draw their attention to the way our perspective or point of view changes what we see:

"What can you do with a small paper umbrella?"

"What can you pretend?"

"What can you build?"

"What do you see when you look at the umbrella from the top?"

"What do you see when you look at the umbrella from the side?"

"How might you build something that looks like what we saw in *Yellow Umbrella*?"

"Can you build a street? How?"

"Can you build a playground? How?"

"Can you build train tracks? Or stairs?"

"Try standing above your building and look down. Tell me about what you see."

Next Steps

If your school is located in or near a tall building, consider taking the children on a special walk to an upper floor where they can look out the windows and view the smaller buildings, the streets, and the people below. If possible, do this on a rainy day when they might see people carrying umbrellas.

Ask the children, "What do you see? How is the view from up here different from what you see when you're down on the ground?" Take photos or invite children to draw what they see. Later, compare your photos and drawings to those in *Yellow Umbrella*.

Look for other picture books that have illustrations from a bird's-eye view. Another great book is *Look Up!* by Jin-Ho Jung (2018). You may also begin to notice that many of your favorite picture books include some illustrations from a bird's-eye view, such as the images of Boston in Robert McCloskey's (2016) classic *Make Way for Ducklings*.

Project 15

BILLY GOAT BRIDGE

"Three Billy Goats Gruff" is a well-known fairy tale that provides an architectural challenge. In this story three goats take turns crossing a bridge guarded by a troll. The bridge itself is the primary setting of the story—and the wonderful opportunity for construction inspiration.

A bridge is an iconic architectural structure and a classic civil engineering challenge. A bridge must be strong enough to safely carry travelers across an expanse of space or over water or other obstacles. A strong bridge must be balanced and symmetrical.

Materials

Bridge construction projects inspired by "Three Billy Goats Gruff" can be built with any of the materials described in this book: blocks and LEGO bricks, found items, recyclables, and wood. If possible, provide children with small toy animal figures that can serve as the goats.

Provocations and Invitations

The story itself can serve as an inspiration and provocation for bridge building. Acting out the story, especially the clip-clopping across the bridge, deepens children's understanding and interest in the story and in the setting. Here are some versions recommended for preschoolers:

While any toy animals can play the roles of the Billy Goats Gruff, it's nice to have some goat toys on hand for this activity.

The Three Billy Goats Gruff by Mary Finch (2001)

The Three Billy Goats Gruff by Paul Galdone (1981)

The Three Billy Goats Gruff by Rebecca Hu-Van Wright (2014)

Considerations

If small toy figures are available to serve as goats, introduce the animals to the children as "the Three Billy Goats Gruff" and invite them to construct a bridge that will be strong enough to hold even the biggest billy goat.

Building a strong and balanced bridge usually involves some trial and error. If the bridge is not strong enough or big enough to hold the billy goats, it might topple over. Encourage children to test their bridges by acting out the story with the toys. If the bridge falls down, explain that this is all part of the engineering experience: "How smart you were to test the bridge first. Now we know that it must be stronger and bigger to support the billy goats."

Big Ideas and Open-Ended Questions

As children construct bridges, ask questions and make observations that draw their attention to the architectural and engineering features of bridges:

"How will you build your bridge?"

"How will you make it strong?"

"How will you know if your bridge is strong enough to hold the billy goats?"

"How high will you make your bridge? How long will you make it?"

"Show me where the troll will hide. And where will the billy goats enter the bridge? Where will they go next?"

Next Steps

As the conversations and explorations of bridges progress, some children may be interested in finding new ways to test the strength of their bridges. Gather some heavy objects, such as thick books, that can be placed on a bridge to test its strength. Ask children to estimate how many heavy books their bridge can hold. Then test the strength of the structure by placing the books on the bridge. If the bridge breaks, invite the children to rebuild it and find new ways to make it stronger. Then test it again!

CHAPTER 6

Maps and Blueprints

As digital technology advances, our relationship with maps—as learners and as navigators of the physical world—has changed. Today we use global positioning systems and digital assistants, such as Siri and Alexa, to help us get from place to place. Gone are the days when we carried accordion-like road maps in our cars and asked strangers on street corners for directions.

There's no harm in exposing children, in moderation, to digital tools and artificial intelligence for navigation. However, children will learn with more autonomy and creativity if you balance virtual experiences with physical and tangible ones.

Even in the digital age, children learning to navigate their world still need experiences with paper maps. They need them for many of the same reasons children learning to read still need books on paper. It's important, too, to offer children experiences with drawing and reading paper blueprints, which represent real buildings and structures.

Despite our digital advancements, children need tangible, physical, sensory experiences in order to learn and understand new ideas with depth and complexity. A book about architecture and young children would not be complete without a discussion of maps and blueprints. This chapter will help you unlock children's ability to capture their ideas about buildings and construction on paper.

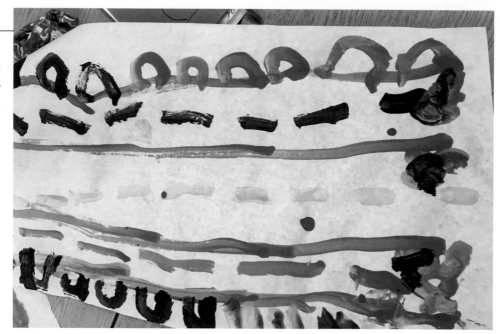

Young children are just beginning to understand the concept of maps, yet they are often inspired to create drawings that share map characteristics.

The Magic of Maps

Personally, I am drawn to the aesthetic beauty of maps. When I was a child, my favorite books were those that included an illustrated map of the story's setting. I was particularly enchanted by E. H. Shephard's illustrated map of the Hundred Acre Wood in the opening pages of A. A. Milne's (1988) *Winnie the Pooh*. Another favorite was Jules Feiffer's map of the Kingdom of Wisdom on the endpapers of Norton Juster's (1989) *The Phantom Tollbooth*.

Often the difference between a "drawing" and a "map" is simply one of perspective. An essential characteristic of a map is the bird's-eye view perspective. As discussed in chapter 5, a bird's-eye view allows us to consider an object as if we were looking at it from above. This change in perspective can be challenging for young children to grasp, but we can scaffold their learning.

Children need inspiration and opportunities to draw maps. I've frequently observed that when children are given graph paper, they will often choose to draw buildings, patterns, lines, and symmetrical designs that are either intentionally created as maps or that resemble maps. Simply providing a quality children's atlas, such Aleksandra Mizielinska and Daniel Mizielinski's (2013) beautiful *Maps*, will likely spark some inventive drawing and interesting classroom conversations.

2D Blueprints, 3D Buildings

A blueprint is a drawing or plan for a structure—essentially a map of a building. The *blue* in *blueprint* comes from the historic practice of using light-sensitive paper, which has white lines on a blue background, to reproduce technical drawings. Although this reproduction process is rarely used today, the term *blueprint* is still commonly used to describe any type of architectural plan, including those created using digital design tools.

An architectural structure, whether a child's simple block tower or a complex Manhattan skyscraper, is a solid. In terms of geometry, it exists in a three-dimensional (3D) space. A drawing or blueprint on a piece of paper, in contrast, exists in a two-dimensional (2D) space. As described in Euclidean geometry, it exists on a plane, or flat surface.

When children move from working in 3D (building a house made of blocks) to working in 2D (using paper and pencil to draw a picture or blueprint of their block house), they utilize different tools and different motor skills. They also utilize different cognitive skills, expanding their thinking in new ways.

When we are challenged to represent a 3D structure in 2D, our minds must interpret and imagine the shapes and architecture in new ways. The same is true when children are invited to draw a 2D blueprint and then build the 3D structure. Moving from 3D to 2D as well as from 2D to 3D involves an exciting cognitive process that sparks deep learning and creativity.

This type of learning, which involves creating multiple representations of an idea or object, is at the heart of the Reggio Emilia approach to early childhood education. Reggio-inspired educators call this concept "the hundred languages of children." As mentioned in the introduction to this book, Loris Malaguzzi, one of the founders of the infant-toddler centers and preschools of Reggio Emilia, famously wrote, "The child has a hundred languages, a hundred thoughts, a hundred ways of thinking, of playing, of speaking" (Malaguzzi 1993, 3).

Malaguzzi recognized that when children are invited to explore and represent their ideas in new ways, using new tools and new methods, they will notice something different with each new representation. They will learn to pay attention to the beautiful and interesting details in their world. Blueprints, floor plans, and illustrations of architectural structures offer a similar aesthetic as maps. They have a geometric order, often with beautiful patterns and symmetry.

A Classroom Map Experience

Mike Pribbenow is a teacher at Preschool of the Arts, a Reggio-inspired program in Madison, Wisconsin. He's a talented freelance artist as well as an early childhood educator. He observed that the children in his class enjoyed playing a form of hide-and-seek. One child would hide a toy on the playground, and another child would find it.

Mike offered the children a new element to the game: he would draw a map of the playground, and the children could use it to find the hidden toy. They could use it like a treasure map to mark the spot where a toy was hidden.

So Mike drew a map. As the children watched him draw, they contributed ideas about which landmarks to include, such as the monkey bars and the sandbox. He sketched each of these landmarks as simple icons the children could easily "read." Later Mike laminated the map so the children could use a dry-erase marker to tag the location of the hidden toy.

The children became so enthusiastic about the playground map that Mike expanded their mapmaking collaborations to include the whole school. Starting with his own classroom, the Sunshine Room, he visited each of the fourteen classrooms and observed the children playing in the space. He then drew a map with landmarks, such as furniture and toys, that children were actively using in meaningful ways. As he worked, he showed the children his maps in progress and asked for their advice and input. In this way he was able to create maps that represented the children's perspective and priorities.

Mike's experience gives us a unique perspective on the many ways children see and think about the physical spaces where they play and learn. This experience also suggests that children are able to understand the concept of maps as 2D representations of a place when we scaffold their learning with conversations and activities that are truly child-centered and steeped in context and meaning.

On page 93 is the map of the Sunshine Room Mike made in collaboration with the Sunshine Room children.

Note the different perspectives in this drawing. Mike drew some of the features from a bird's-eye view (the rectangular rugs), some from a side view (child's block structure), and some from a more realistic angle (art easel). This combination of perspectives seemed to help scaffold children's understanding of perspective.

Most of us are not as talented as Mike in our ability to draw freely and spontaneously, but we can all take advantage of opportunities to help children make meaningful connections between their 3D physical world and a 2D map

The maps that Mike created with the children are intentionally drawn from dual perspectives. Some elements are shown as if viewed from the side, and some are shown as if viewed from above, which exposes children to multiple perspectives.

or blueprint. When children learn about maps and blueprints they develop important spatial reasoning skills. They also learn math concepts related to measurement and scale.

This map of the Sunshine classroom shows the geography of the room as well as the children's favorite activities that were happening on the day the map was made.

Maps and Blueprints in Your Classroom

To encourage projects and exploration, you may wish to set up a classroom workspace, either permanent or temporary, featuring maps and blueprints. Ask an architectural firm or construction company in your community if they will donate unwanted blueprints to your school. Most architects and engineers will be delighted to contribute to your STEM curriculum. (Note: some school-supply companies sell rugs preprinted with roads and other map-like landmarks, but I've observed that the novelty of these rugs quickly wears off. Children tend to be much more intrigued by actual maps and blueprints.)

In addition to providing actual maps and blueprints, you can also encourage children to create their own. Have a ready supply of graph paper in various sizes and textures, sharpened pencils, fine-tip markers, rulers, and tracing tools. A set of rubber stamps can be used to create icons or landmarks on maps and blueprints.

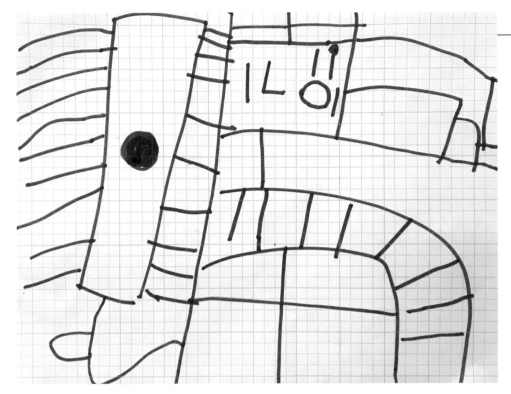

Teachable Moments

The projects in this chapter provide specific opportunities to incorporate maps and blueprints into your classroom activities. However, you can also keep your eyes and ears open for spontaneous teachable moments throughout the day. For example, a child might say, "My mommy works at the mall. She drives her car to work." This comment can inspire a conversation in which you challenge the child to put her thoughts and ideas about places into words. You could ask, "Is the mall far away or is it nearby? How do you know?" or "Where does your mommy go when she drives to work?" or "If we wanted to drive or walk to the mall from here, which direction would we go?" Young children will find these questions very challenging, but you may be surprised by how much they understand and how well they can communicate about their sense of direction and orientation using words and gestures.

You can take these teachable moments even further. For the example described above, you can help the child create a simple map on paper that shows just two landmarks: home and the mall. The child can draw a line between the two points to represent the streets her mommy takes to drive to work.

You could also invite the child to add her preschool as another landmark and draw additional lines of connection.

The child's active role in connecting these locations on paper will not only support her cognitive development but will likely also support her social and emotional development as well. The process of creating the map may help the child feel more secure and less anxious about being away from her mommy. She now has control over how she represents her and her mommy's locations, and the lines she draws on the page give her the power to connect to her mommy in a meaningful way.

Integrating Digital and Tangible Experiences

As mentioned earlier, maps and blueprints are now different in the digital age. Therefore, it's important to balance digital with tangible experiences.

For the child who created the map showing her home and the mall, give her time to deeply engage with her map, then invite her to compare it to a digital map on a phone, tablet, or computer. Ask questions that promote critical thinking about maps and technology: "How is your map different from the map on the computer? How is it the same? Which map do you like better? Why?"

Technology can provide unique perspective, which is a key aspect of both maps and blueprints. One interesting development in technology that seems to have an impact on how we view our world is drone photography and videography. As mentioned earlier, imagining a bird's-eye view can be challenging for young children, but as the use of drones becomes more common, children are exposed more frequently to this view from above.

Recently, Tapio Snellman, a London-based filmmaker, collaborated with students in Folkestone, Kent, to make a film using drones. The film captured unique views of themselves and their urban environment. It's a very beautiful representation of the children in their community. For many of the children, it surely sparked a deep fascination with space and place.

BLOCK FOOTPRINT TRACINGS

In this activity children learn how to create footprints of their own block houses. A footprint is the area of space a building covers. Like blueprints, footprints represent a three-dimensional structure using a two-dimensional medium: paper.

Place a large piece of paper on the floor of the block area (or scale down for a tabletop) and invite children to build their block house on the paper. When they're done building, they can use a marker to trace the outline of their house directly onto the piece of paper. After they remove the blocks, they'll have a tracing of their building—a footprint!

Materials

The basic materials needed for this activity include paper, blocks, pencils, crayons, or washable markers. Your exact materials may differ depending on costs and where you're doing the activity.

If you're working on the floor, supersized graph paper with a one-inch grid works really well. Children often enjoy aligning their structures to the right angles of the grid. However, that kind of paper can be expensive. A less costly way to create the same effect is to draw some gridlines on plain newsprint or poster paper before placing it on the floor.

If working on a tabletop, you can use ordinary graph paper and smaller blocks, such as one-inch cube blocks or Duplo blocks. In addition to markers, pencils and pens could also be used for tracing, as the tabletop is a harder surface.

Provocations and Invitations

A large piece of paper on the floor of the block corner (or on a tabletop) is a great provocation in and of itself. As children gather around, ask them, "What is a footprint? Do you have one?" You can then follow it up with, "Did you know a house can have a footprint too?"

Next, invite children to build houses with blocks on the surface of the paper. As they work, ask open-ended questions that draw their attention to the lines and features of the printed blueprints, such as, "What lines do you see? What do these lines make you think about? What could you build here?"

Considerations

Once they see the large piece of paper on the floor, many children will be eager to start drawing on their own. You may need to explain that they need to do a special activity first. Once they're done, then they'll be welcome to draw on the paper.

Some children may need you to demonstrate or explain what you mean by "tracing" the blocks. Show them how to hold the tip of the marker close to where the block touches the paper and then move the marker so it draws a line around the edges of the block.

This will be a difficult task for most preschoolers. Their lines may not be straight, and they may accidently bump their block structure. Let the children know that learning to trace takes time and that their tracing does not have to be perfect. As a way to practice, some children may enjoy first tracing just one block.

If the paper will be placed on carpet, you may need to coach the children to avoid pressing too hard on the paper, as the marker may poke through. A light touch works best. When tracing on a tabletop, children will be able to press harder and make a firmer line without worry.

After the children have finished tracing, explain that to see their house's footprint, they will need to remove the blocks. Some children may want to keep playing with blocks and check the paper later.

Once the blocks are removed from the paper, look at the tracings together and talk about the lines and shapes. In addition to the concept of footprints, some children may also enjoy learning the word *perimeter* to describe the line that forms the edge or boundary of an area or shape.

Big Ideas and Open-Ended Questions

As children work on tracing their house footprints, ask questions and make observations that draw their attention to the architectural spatial features of their creations:

"Tell me about the house you've built with blocks."

"Tell me about how you made your footprint."

"I see different kinds of lines on your footprint. Why are some long and some short? Why are some curved and some straight?"

"How is a house made with blocks different from a footprint on paper? How is it the same?"

"When you look at your footprint, what do you see?"

Next Steps

It's relatively easy to move from footprints to blueprints. Invite children to add real or imagined details to their tracing, such as inner walls or outdoor landscaping. Ask them to think of the rooms in their house.

Explain to the children that one of the wonderful reasons we create blueprints is so we can remember what we made and build it again. Invite children to save and use their blueprint again as a guide so that they or their friends can build the same house another day.

Children who enjoy tracing their block structures on paper may also enjoy tracing the shadow of their block house on a wall. Place a lamp or projector so it casts a shadow of the house on a wall or piece of furniture. Tape a piece of paper on that surface. Next, show the children how to trace the shadow.

Again, let them know it can take some practice. In addition to the challenge of controlling the marker, there is the added challenge of figuring out how to keep from blocking the light with your own body. In spite of the challenges, many preschool children will be intrigued by the process and willing to give it a try.

Children may also be intrigued by how moving the light source can change the size of the shadow. When you move the light farther away from the block structure, the shadow will appear to grow! Simply using a projector to create shadows on the wall will add excitement and complexity to children's block building, whether they stop to trace the shadows or not.

Project 17

SCHOOL MAP

Mike Pribbenow's story (see pages 92–93) demonstrates that young children are eager to create maps of their school, playground, and classrooms, especially when the process is collaborative and meaningful to them. You can capture this same excitement in your classroom as well—even if you don't have Mike's artistic skill.

Most preschool children have not yet developed the cognitive and fine-motor skills necessary to independently create a map of their school. Despite the challenge, many Reggio-inspired and project-based teachers would insist it's exactly the type of project you can turn into an exciting collaborative learning opportunity.

Making a school map is within the children's zone of proximal development (ZPD), a concept articulated by child psychologist Lev Vygotsky. ZPD is the space between what a child can do independently and what a child can do with assistance (Knestrick 2012). To create a school map with a group of preschool children, your role as teacher is to scaffold learning. You need to provide enough direction and assistance to allow them to engage in meaningful ways. This means you may need to draw the footprint, make a copy for each child, and invite them to add features and landmarks on their own. Another option is to draw and label a single classroom map based on input from the children, as Mike did. You may also choose to combine these two strategies in your own way.

Materials

As challenging as this project may be, it's also as simple as drawing on paper. At the very least, you'll need plain or graph paper plus pencils and markers. Rulers can help with straight lines, especially if you're using plain paper. A clipboard or poster board can help you bring your map with you as you move about the school.

Provocations and Invitations

Most early childhood classrooms have an emergency evacuation route map posted somewhere near the door. As a provocation, share these maps with the children. Help them see that the map is a 2D picture of the school. Then ask, "Would you like to make our own map of the school?" If possible, make paper copies of the evacuation map and give one to each child. Invite the children to draw and add details to their own map, each in their own way.

Considerations

As they work on the maps, the children will need to see, and even touch, the spaces they are thinking and talking about. So place the maps in progress on clipboards and invite the children to carry them as they walk around the school. Or if you are working collaboratively on a single map, mount the map on a sturdy piece of poster board and carry it with you. Look at the space together and "survey" where landmarks are located.

Don't worry about measuring actual distances. At this point the most important spatial-reasoning task is exploring the positions of objects or features (doors, stairs, and so forth) relative to one another. For example, it's not important to know that the stairs are twenty feet from the door. However, it is important to know that the stairs are at the front of the building, near the main entrance door.

Invite the children to take turns sketching these types of details onto the draft of their school maps. Listen carefully as children discuss their maps and write down their details and comments. Even if children are working on their own individual maps, you may still want to create one large classroom map on which you document the learning process by writing down some of the children's ideas, comments, and questions.

Big Ideas and Open-Ended Questions

As children work on the maps, ask questions and make observations that draw their attention to the building features and their relative positions:

"What should we include on our maps?"

"How will we know if we've put things in the right places?"

"What do you see when you walk in the door?"

"Why might we need a map of our school? Who will use it? What will they use it for?"

"What are the most important places in our school? How can we show those places on our map?"

Next Steps

Once the individual maps and/or the classroom map is complete, you can help the children understand how maps function in our everyday lives. Encourage children to use the school maps for various purposes, such as playing treasure-hunt games or giving tours of the school to parents or visitors.

The collaborative school map can be a living project that you continually revise and adapt as children gain new understandings of the space and the ways to represent it on a piece of paper. Create multiple copies of the building footprint and invite children to work on new versions of the map.

Project 18

DOGHOUSES

This activity does not involve making maps or blueprints; rather, its purpose is to inspire children to think about an important concept in maps and blueprints: scale. Scale is the ratio of size as represented in maps, blueprints, plans, or models (such as model trains). On a map you'll often find a small explanatory key that describes the scale in words or symbols. For example, one inch might represent one mile.

We can introduce young children to the concept of scale by focusing on the broad differences between big things and little things. For example, a preschool child can understand that some dogs are big, and some dogs are small. A big dog needs big things, and a small dog needs small things.

In this activity children will be invited to build a big doghouse for a big dog and a small doghouse for a small dog. This construction project will challenge children to think about scale as they determine the appropriate size of each house.

Materials

You will need two toy dogs, one big and one little. Ideally, the big dog will be approximately twice the size of the small dog. For example, if the small dog is three inches tall, the big dog should ideally be around six inches tall. This exact scale is not necessary, but there should be a noticeable difference in size.

To build the doghouses, you can use blocks, LEGO bricks, or cardboard. Choose construction materials that the children are already familiar with and enjoy using.

Provocations and Invitations

If possible, introduce this activity by displaying or showing real dog items, such as collars or dishes. Ask them to guess the size of the dog that might use each of these items. Invite the children to show you the size of the dog with their hands. Ask, "If the dog that uses this collar were here on this rug, how tall would he be? Show me with your hands."

Next, introduce the children to the two toy dogs you've selected for this activity. Ask the children, "What do you notice about these two dogs? How are they different?" Tell the children that these dogs need a house to live in. Invite the children to build a house that is just right for each dog.

Considerations

Allow children to design and build the houses in any style they choose. It will be interesting to see if they build the same type of house for each dog or if they build two styles of houses.

Once the houses are complete, take turns testing the structures. Place the big toy dog inside each child's big house and the small toy dog inside the small house. Do the dogs fit? If the dogs don't fit, invite the children to make changes to the houses until they are satisfied.

Children will be able to recognize when the house is too small; the dog will not be able to enter the house. A house that's too big, however, may be harder

These simple LEGO structures demonstrate the idea that a bigger dog needs a bigger house.

to recognize. Ask the children, "How much room does a dog need?" and "If you were this dog, would you feel cozy and happy in a house this size?"

Big Ideas and Open-Ended Questions

As children build the doghouses, ask questions that draw their attention to the size and scale of their structures:

"How will you make a house for the big dog?"

"How will you make a house for the little dog?"

"How is building a house for a big dog different from building a house for a little dog?"

"How will you know if your house is the right size?"

Next Steps

As children explore the sizes of the dogs and the houses, you may want to introduce measuring tools, such as rulers, and standard units of measurement, such as inches. Some children may already be familiar with these tools and terms.

It may be as simple as measuring the houses and/or dogs and comparing the numbers. Or you may want to invite the children to help you create a sign or poster that shows the size and scale of the toy dogs. The children could help draw an image of each dog that is the dog's actual size.

CHAPTER 7

Extended Projects

The ideas, provocations, and projects offered in this book are each valuable as individual experiences with minimal time commitment. At the same time, any one of these experiences could become the first step in a much longer and more complex journey—the start of an extended project that takes place over time.

In general the projects described in this chapter are more appropriate for older preschool children and kindergarteners. Certainly, though, some younger preschoolers might also have the attention span and deep curiosity to participate in extended projects.

Long-term and extended projects can often be found in emergent curriculum classrooms. With an emergent curriculum approach, teachers develop their curriculum in response to children's emerging interests and inquiries. And whenever children's interests stretch and deepen beyond a single learning experience, extended projects naturally unfold.

The Reggio Emilia approach is one example of an emergent curriculum process. Reggio-inspired teachers observe children's interests, provide provocations that spark deeper conversations and explorations, and facilitate the development of projects that engage children in representing their ideas using multiple media (i.e., the hundred languages).

Another example of emergent curriculum is the project approach, as defined by Lilian Katz and developed by educators such as Judy Harris-Helm. In the project approach, the teacher identifies a topic of interest and facilitates the development of a large collaborative project. This becomes the centerpiece of the curriculum unit.

What all these approaches have in common is that the teachers are responsive to children's interests and that there is a significant amount of collaboration. Architectural projects, such as those described in this book, often bring a group of children together to design and build something. These types of activities are particularly well suited to emergent curriculum practices and can be easily adapted for extended exploration.

Older preschoolers and kindergarteners are developing the patience and skill to collaborate on larger, more detailed construction projects.

The Essentials: Time and Space

In the world of early childhood education, an extended or "long-term" project is really any project that lasts more than a single lesson or session. Given the way we live our lives and educate our children, we so often find ourselves rushing through the day—and the curriculum.

It's hard to slow down and let children take the lead, but we must continually remind ourselves that young children need time to think and learn. They need to revisit ideas again and again to grow their understanding.

For this reason we need to advocate on children's behalf, reminding families and stakeholders of the importance to slow down. Formally adopting an emergent approach and building your schedule around project-based learning will help you make time for child-centered learning.

In addition to time, children need space. In particular, extended collaborative construction projects often require a great deal of space. A LEGO city, for example, is a project that can't easily be put away. A project isn't truly "extended" if children need to deconstruct their city at the end of the day and then reconstruct it at the beginning of the next. Rather, the city needs to stay intact so children can continue their progress. (And it needs to stay safe from accidental or intentional "deconstruction.")

Strategies for reserving and protecting space for projects will vary, depending on each school and classroom. Here are some ideas to consider:

- Setting aside one corner of the room for extended projects
- Having children build their construction project on a large piece of plywood or a tabletop so you can move it to another room or storage area
- Using covered outdoor spaces (e.g., porches, pavilions, and so forth) for extended projects, as weather permits
- Utilizing shared spaces such as hallways and lobbies

Developmentally Appropriate Research Practices

When given time and space, an extended project can take on a life of its own, branching into areas beyond its original scope. In some cases an extended construction project will inspire questions, which in turn inspire a related research project. In an early childhood classroom, *research* can refer to activities and conversations that allow children to learn more about a particular topic, question, or idea.

But how do we teach research skills to prereaders and beginning readers? This is where developmentally appropriate research practices, such as inquiry-based learning, are helpful.

Inquiry-based learning is an approach in which teachers shape the curriculum and develop extended projects in response to children's questions. With this approach teachers must have the disposition and tools to help children conduct research.

For example, when I was a preschool teacher I had a group of children who were fascinated by the water faucets in the bathroom. When washing their hands, they would often talk about the pipes visible under the sink. One child said there were alligators and snakes living in the pipes. Another child said the pipes sucked the water up from Lake Michigan.

Sometimes the children would ask me questions about the pipes. I realized I didn't know enough about plumbing and city water systems to give them accurate answers. We needed to do some research.

Let's look at how you might lead children in an inquiry-based project based on this example. The first step is documenting the children's questions. This can be done through simple dictation. Invite the children to voice all their questions (e.g., "Do snakes live in pipes?" and "How do the pipes make the water hot and cold?"), and then write them down.

After reviewing the large sample of questions, you can then help the group focus on one broad or important question to research. In this case the broad question that ties all the children's questions together is "How do the pipes work?"

Research can now begin as you help children search for the answers to their broad question. Preschool and kindergarten children, however, are not yet ready to conduct independent research using text-based sources. This means you need to model the text-based research process. You can demonstrate how someone can select and use nonfiction and reference books from a library and/or search online for safe and trusted sources of accurate information.

For example, gather a stack of nonfiction books and ask the children, "Which of these books might contain some interesting information about pipes and plumbing?" The children will likely enjoy looking at the images and photos in these books. They may also ask you to read aloud the titles and text.

As you explore these nonfiction resources, also share with the children how you're deciding what to read and what information is important. For example, tell them, "Here's a picture of a pipe. I'm going to read the words printed below the picture. Maybe these words will tell us something new about how pipes work."

One of the most engaging methods of research for young children is learning from experts. In this case: consulting a plumber. Many professionals, such as plumbers, architects, engineers, and construction workers, would welcome the opportunity to visit a classroom and answer questions about the topics that interest the children.

As you take on extended architectural projects, keep your ears open for the questions that will inevitably pop up along the way. One or more of those questions could present a wonderful opportunity for research, which will only deepen the children's learning experience.

SHIPWRECK HOUSE

The inspiration for this shipwreck house activity comes from the children's book *The Sailor Dog* by Margaret Wise Brown and illustrated by Garth Williams (2001). In this story Sailor Dog, the spunky and resourceful protagonist, is stranded on a desert island after a shipwreck.

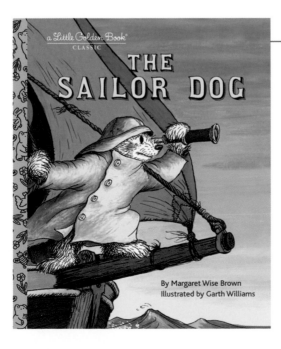

Garth Williams's illustrations in *The Sailor Dog* may inspire children to create their own house out of odds and ends.

As a child, I was absolutely fascinated by one particular page from the book (originally published in 1953). It was an illustration of the industrious Sailor Dog building a shelter out of whatever he could find on the island—the wood and various pieces of his broken ship, as well as driftwood and rocks found along the shore. I loved the idea of being able to make yourself a house using only whatever you happened to find. Sometimes limitations spark creativity.

This is the idea behind the *Ready, Set, Design!* framework developed by the Cooper Hewitt Smithsonian Design Museum. In a *Ready, Set, Design!* activity a group (adults and children alike) is given a small paper bag filled with a limited number of building materials, such as craft sticks, foil, and tape. The group is then given a challenge or prompt, such as "Design something that helps people stay safe." Working together with a limited mix of materials sparks creativity for both adults and children.

In the same spirit, this project invites children to imagine being shipwrecked on an island and building a house out of a limited and novel mix of construction materials. Working together in pairs will spark creativity and provide valuable opportunities for social development.

While this project can be presented as a single experience, the challenge—and fun—deepens when it's stretched over the long term. New materials can suddenly "wash ashore" each day. This prompts the children to rethink their designs and incorporate these new pieces.

The *Ready, Set, Design!* framework calls for a combination of three types of open-ended materials, such as pipe cleaners, clothespins, and Popsicle sticks.

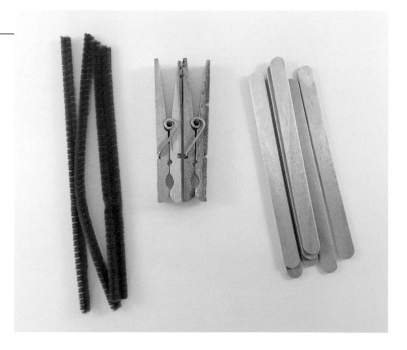

Materials

Any variety of materials will create a unique building challenge. An ideal mix for preschoolers would include some kind of base construction materials (such as wood scraps and cardboard), something that will help things stick together (such as tape and clay), and something to add features or decorations (such as sticks and pieces of wire or string).

Keep the "shipwreck" concept in mind. It's easy to build a house with blocks, but the point here is to build with materials that are more challenging.

Keep in mind, too, that you'll need to provide new and different items each day as the project continues. Perhaps one day you'll offer pebbles. The next, pipe cleaners. And the next, bottle caps from the recycling bin. Children will need to think about their project in new and evolving ways.

Provocations and Invitations

The Sailor Dog can be used as a provocation for this activity. After sharing the book, direct the children to the extended-project area (see suggestions above), where the materials will be waiting in prepared bags.

Encourage them to imagine they're like Sailor Dog—they're stranded on an island and need to build a house. Offer a bag to each pair of children and invite them to build a house using only the materials in the bag. Tell them, "We'll work on these houses today and then keep them at school in case we have new ideas. Maybe some new materials will wash ashore tomorrow. Let's see what happens!"

Considerations

For preschoolers, this activity works well when children work together in pairs. Collaborating in a larger group is a challenge better reserved for older grades.

On the first day of the project, simply offer the materials and see what happens. Usually some children will be very engaged and eager to build. Others may struggle. Allow the children to leave the materials on a tray or plate to "save" for another time.

When the children return the next day, encourage them to check on their in-progress houses. Offer new materials, either in individual bags, as before, or simply set out in a tray or box. The children will be delighted by the surprise and eager to discover what items they can incorporate next.

As the project continues, some children will likely be very eager to work with the new items, and others may need some encouragement to add to a house they think is "done." Keep in mind that most children are not accustomed to this kind of flexible and open-ended design thinking. You may need to serve as a role model, demonstrating how new materials can be incorporated into a house that is still "under construction."

Big Ideas and Open-Ended Questions

As children build, ask questions and make observations that help them collaborate and think creatively. Each day you can repeat these same questions and prompts as children discover the new materials that have washed ashore.

"Look at these materials. What do you see?"

"How might these materials build a house?"

"What are some ideas you each have for building a house?"

"What ideas are you trying first? Why?"

"What else can you try?"

Next Steps

After several days of building their shipwreck houses, the children will likely want to play with them. Help children find or make little people or animals that can live in their houses.

Because the houses will likely be grouped together in the extended-project area, encourage the children to play collaboratively, turning the area into a shipwreck village. Perhaps they will want to build roads between the houses. In that case, think of novel materials that will once again inspire the children to build in creative and resourceful ways.

Project 20

MODEL PLAYGROUND

Children are intimately familiar with what works and what doesn't in play spaces and playground equipment. In short, they're experts on playground design. Yet how often do we consult children in the design and construction of actual playgrounds? Not often enough, is the answer from Mara Mintzer. She is the founder of Growing Up Boulder, a child-and-youth-friendly city program that actively includes children's and teen's voices in decisions about parks and other initiatives. In her popular TED Talk titled "How Kids Can Help Design Cities" (2017), Mintzer makes the case that children should have a say in not only the design of parks and playgrounds but in all urban planning.

How deeply are children involved in decisions about their play spaces at your school and in your community? In this extended collaborative project, you can invite children to imagine an ideal playground and bring it to life as a model. It's an endeavor to implement with care, intention, and time.

In the first phase, invite the children to think about the features, such as equipment and landscaping, they'd like in a playground. In the second phase, encourage them to draw, share, and discuss their ideas on paper. In the third phase, prompt them to build a 3D model of their playground with various construction materials.

Once the project is done, you can share the model playground with parents and community members. It might just spark action to make their playground a reality.

Materials

In the second phase of the project, you'll need paper and pencils as the children capture their ideas in 2D. Once children are ready to truly build and create their ideas in the third phase, provide them with a variety of 3D construction materials: cardboard tubes, plastic containers, wire, pipe cleaners or chenille stems, craft sticks, clay, tape, construction paper, cardboard, and more. Natural found items, such as stones and sticks, can represent landscaping features.

As a truly collaborative community project, all the children will work together on one playground model. You may, however, choose to have children work in small groups to create several model playgrounds. For each playground model, provide a large piece of cardboard, foam board, or poster board so children have a flat, solid surface for building. This will also make it easier to move the in-progress playgrounds to the extended-project area.

Provocations and Invitations

The provocation for this project is also its first phase. You can start by asking children to evaluate their school's playground or a public play area they visit often. Ask them to point out the things they like and don't like. Document their feedback with photos and dictated text. Pose questions such as, "When you play on a playground, what are your favorite things to do?" "What parts of this playground do you like best?" "Are there parts of this playground that you don't like?" and "If you could build a playground, what would you put in it?"

Considerations

With its many phases, this project is about advance planning. This can be challenging for young children, especially those who think with their hands.

Be patient and responsive to the pace, needs, and interests of the children. Anticipate how you might be able to scaffold learning and lend a helping hand. (They may need help with tricky tasks like folding, cutting, and taping.)

The second phase of the project might be easier if you've completed the classroom map project in chapter 6. The children will be more familiar, then, with concepts on representing places and spaces on paper. This will help them as they envision where they want to place various features of their ideal playground.

Throughout the process provide opportunities for the children to revisit their projects to observe, think, discuss, and make revisions as needed. For instance, perhaps the children will want to create a "rough draft" of the model playground, arranging and rearranging pieces, before they create a more permanent final version. The larger goal here is to introduce the idea that the things we make can be planned, discussed, and revised.

Model playgrounds can be constructed out of a variety of craft materials.

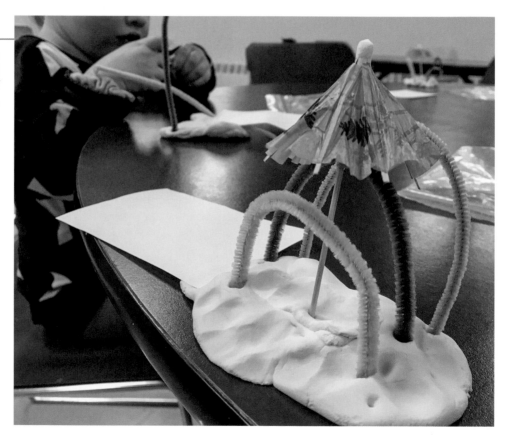

Big Ideas and Open-Ended Questions

As children work on their playground design, ask questions and make observations that draw their attention to the ways their design supports their vision for an ideal playground:

"What part of the playground will you make first/next?"

"How will you make it?"

"Do you need ideas from a friend or a teacher?"

"If this were a real playground, what would it be like to play here?"

"Does this look like what you were imagining in your head?"

"How can we make this playground model even better?"

Next Steps

The children's playground model could be used as a tool for advocating for child-centered play spaces. The children could show their design to school leaders or send pictures of their design to city planners. For additional resources about child-centered urban planning, visit the website for the Child in the City Foundation (2020).

Project 21

LEGO CITY

When I was a program coordinator at Northwestern University's Center for Talent Development, we offered a weeklong summer class called LEGO Architecture. It was loads of fun. Children spent an entire week designing and building a variety of creative structures.

One summer we added another interesting element to the class. We changed the name to LEGO Metropolis, and we challenged the children to work together throughout the week on a common goal: creating a LEGO city.

This added an entirely new level of fun and creativity. The children were not only talking and planning (and sometimes arguing) about their city, but they were also thinking about scale so their buildings would be uniform in size. It wouldn't work for one person's single-story house to be ten LEGO bricks tall and the next person's to be twenty-five. The class had to decide together how tall a single-story house or building would be, and then everyone needed to think about that scale when building their structures. (The doghouse project in chapter 6 is a good introduction to the concept of scale.)

This LEGO city incorporates both standard LEGO (colors) and specialized architecture LEGO (plain white).

The LEGO Metropolis class has been taught for eight years now in many different locations throughout Chicago. Each time, the children create a completely different and unique city.

Materials

To build a sprawling LEGO city, you need an ample supply of classic LEGO bricks. (See chapter 1 for a discussion on LEGO sets.) We probably used about ten thousand LEGO bricks in each LEGO Metropolis class. You will also need a large workspace that does not have to be cleaned up each day.

Provocations and Invitations

Most children need little provocation when there's a bin of LEGO bricks waiting for them. To help children focus on working together to build a LEGO city, however, share images of skylines and cityscapes. Possible sources for these images can be found in the following books:

Skylines of New York by Richard Berenholtz (2020)

New Architecture New York by Pavel Bendov (2017)

Chicago: Classic Photographs edited by Richard Cahan (2017)

Considerations

The LEGO Metropolis class was a summer enrichment course in which children focused intensely on one topic for the entire week. In an ordinary preschool or kindergarten class, the pace will be much different.

Begin by setting aside the space for the city to grow, offer the provocation, then invite children to work together on just one building: a house, a school, or perhaps the town hall. This works even if only a few children are interested at first.

When that anchor building is complete and placed in the space, ask children to think about what else people need in a city. Ask children questions such as, "Where will people live, work, play, and shop? How will they get from one place to another?"

Let the planning and building of the other structures come from these conversations and ideas. Remember, though, to help the children build with scale in mind. Challenge them to use that first building as a measurement of scale for the rest of the city. As in the doghouse project, remind them to think about the differences in small buildings and big buildings.

Big Ideas and Open-Ended Questions

As children build, ask questions and make observations that draw their attention to urban infrastructure and the meaningful connections between the buildings and landmarks in the city:

"If someone lives here, how will they get to work?"

"What if someone is sick and needs to see a doctor? Where will they go?"

"What if someone uses a wheelchair? How will they get from place to place?"

"How will the people in this city get their water and electricity?"

"Which areas of your city are the busiest? Which parts are quietest? Why?"

"If you lived in this city, what would you like best about it?"

Next Steps

This project connects well with the mapmaking ideas discussed in chapter 6. Invite children to make an illustrated map of their city. If possible, take a photo of their city from above and help the children use that image as a guide for their map.

Children who are especially interested in city maps may enjoy looking at *Great City Maps: A Historical Journey through Maps, Plans, and Paintings* (DK 2016).

Time to Play!

When young architects build structures out of blocks and other kinds of construction materials, they are creating something out of nothing. In a space that was once empty now stands something tangible and solid. For many children this creative and collaborative process is deeply satisfying.

As an early childhood educator, I feel that the most significant value of block and construction play stems from the ways it provides a window into children's minds and hearts. When children build they are making their learning, thinking, and feelings visible in ways that words and conversations can't always communicate. Once we are open to "reading" a child's structure, we can begin to interpret their play and understand the child more deeply.

If you are inspired by concepts of architecture and construction, the children will also be inspired. There are no wrong answers. There are no paths that are not worth traveling. When you begin to play and build, the children will begin to play and build. Pick up a block and place it on the floor. Then add another. See? You've already begun.

Recommended Resources

Architecture and Engineering

Amag! The Architecture Magazine for Children (https://a-magazine.org)

The American Institute of Architects (www.aia.org)

Architecture and Education (https://architectureandeducation.org)

Chicago Architecture Center (www.architecture.org)

The Guardian, "How to Teach Architecture" (www.theguardian.com/education/2016/jun/06/how-to-teach-architecture)

EarthshipsGlobal Biotecture (www.earthshipglobal.com)

National Science Foundation: Engineering Classroom Resources for Teachers (www.nsf.gov/news/classroom/engineering.jsp)

Sistema Lupo (http://sistemalupo.ferminblanco.com/en)

LEGO

The LEGO Architect by Tom Alphin (No Starch Press, 2015): Text, concepts, and terminology are intended for older children, but the photos and illustrations can serve as inspiration for preschoolers.

LEGO Education (https://education.lego.com/en-us)

LEGO Education—Early Learning (https://education.lego.com/en-us/preschool/intro)

LEGO Foundation—Learning through Play (www.legofoundation.com/en/what-we-do/research-centre)

Architecture Organizations

The American Institute of Architects (www.aia.org/about)

Consejo Superior de los Colegios de Arquitectos de España (www.cscae.com)

Royal Institute of British Architects (RIBA) (www.architecture.com)

Suomen ArkkitehtiliittoFinish Association of Architects (SAFA) (www.safa.fi/en)

Architecture Schools and Programs for Children

Finland: Arkki School of Architecture for Children and Youth (http://arkki.net)

Germany: Architektur für Kinder (www.architekturfuerkinder.ch)

Bavarian Chamber of Architects (www.byak.de/veranstaltungen /architektur-fuer-kinder-und-jugendliche.html)

Japan: Ito Juku (http://itojuku.or.jp/about/english)

Spain: Arkitente (www.arkitente.org)

Chiquitectos (www.chiquitectos.com)

United States: Chicago Architecture Center (www.architecture.org/teach -learn/families)

Portland Architects in Schools (www.af-oregon.org/architects-in-schools)

United Kingdom: Designing with Children (http://designingwithchildren.net)

Engaging Places: Architecture and the Built Environment as a Learning Resource

Little Architect: The Architectural Association in the UK Primary Schools (http://littlearchitect.aaschool.ac.uk)

The Royal Institute of British Architects Schools Programme (www.architecture .com/education-cpd-and-careers/learning/schools-programme)

Architecture Books for Children

Architecture according to Pigeons by Speck Lee Tailfeather (Phaidon Press, 2013)

Building Big by David Macaulay (HMH Books for Young Readers, 2004)

City by David Macaulay (HMH Books for Young Readers, 1983)

DK Annotated Guide—Architecture: The World's Greatest Buildings Explored and Explained by Neil Stevenson (DK, 1997)

The Dolls' House Fairy by Jane Ray (Candlewick Press, 2010)

Dreaming Up: A Celebration of Building by Christy Hale (Lee & Lowe, 2012)

Fix That Clock by Kurt Cyrus (HMH Books for Young Readers, 2019)

The Future Architect's Handbook by Barbara Beck (Schiffer, 2014)

The Little Gardener by Emily Hughes (Flying Eye Books, 2018)

Pyramid by David Macaulay (HMH Books for Young Readers, 1982)

Raise the Roof by Anastasia Suen (Viking, 2003)

Round Buildings, Square Buildings, and Buildings That Wiggle Like a Fish by Philip M. Isaacson (Knopf, 2011)

Steven Caney's Ultimate Building Book by Steven Caney (Running Press, 2006)

The Story of Buildings by Patrick Dillon and Stephen Biesty (Candlewick Press, 2014)

Under Every Roof: A Kid's Style and Field Guide to the Architecture of American Houses by Patricia Brown Glenn (Wiley, 2009)

Underground by David Macaulay (HMH Books for Young Readers, 1983)

Who Built That? Skyscrapers by Didier Cornille (Princeton Architectural Press, 2014)

The World Is Not a Rectangle: A Portrait of Architect Zaha Hadid by Jeanette Winter (Beach Lane Books, 2017)

Nonfiction for Adults but Useful to Kids and Teachers

Architecture: Elements, Materials, Form by Francesca Prima (Princeton University Press, 2009)

Building Construction Illustrated by Francis D. K. Ching (Wiley, 2013)

Go: A Kidd's Guide to Graphic Design by Chip Kidd (Workman, 2013)

101 Things I Learned in Architecture School by Matthew Frederick (MIT Press, 2007)

Books for Teachers about Block Play

The Block Book by Elizabeth Hirsch (NAEYC, 1996)

Blocks and Beyond: Strengthening Early Math and Science Skills through Spatial Learning by Mary Jo Pollman (NAEYC, 2011)

Creative Block Play by Rosanne Hansel (Redleaf Press, 2016)

Inventing Kindergarten by Norman Brosterman (Kaleidograph Design, 2014)

References

Barker, Cicely May. 2002. *The Complete Book of the Flower Fairies*. New York: Warner.

Barnett, Mac. 2014. *Sam and Dave Dig a Hole*. New York: Candlewick Press.

Barton, Byron. 1990. *Building a House.* New York: Greenwillow.

Beaty, Andrea. 2007. *Iggy Peck, Architect.* New York: Abrams.

Bendov, Pavel. 2017. *New Architecture New York*. New York: Prestel.

Berenholtz, Richard. 2020. *Skylines of New York*. New York: Welcome Books.

Beskow, Elsa. 1987. *Peter in Blueberry Land*. Edinburgh: Floris Books.

Boisrobert, Anouck, and Louis Rigaud. 2010. *Popville.* New York: Roaring Book Press.

Booth, Tom. 2018. *Day at the Beach*. New York: Jeter Publishing.

Brown, Margaret Wise. 2001. *The Sailor Dog*. New York: Little Golden Book.

Brownell, Jeanine O'Nan, Jie-Qi Chen, Lisa Ginet, Mary Hines-Berry, Rebecca Itzkowich, Donna Johnson, Jennifer McCray. 2014. Erikson Institute Early Math Collaborative, *Big Ideas of Early Mathematics: What Teachers of Young Children Need to Know*. New York: Pearson.

Buntin, Philip. 2019. *Sandcastle*. Crows Nest, Australia: Allen & Unwin.

Burton, Virginia Lee. 1978. *The Little House*. New York: Houghton Mifflin Harcourt.

Cahan, Richard. 2017. *Chicago: Classic Photographs*. Chicago: CityFiles Press.

Child in the City Foundation. 2020. www.childinthecity.org/.

Clark, M. H. 2016. *You Being Here*. Seattle: Compendium.

Common Sense Media. 2017. "The Common Sense Census: Media Use by Kids Age Zero to Eight, 2017." www.commonsensemedia.org/research/the-common-sense-census-media-use-by-kids-age-zero-to-eight-2017.

Cyrus, Kurt. 2016. *Billions of Bricks.* New York: Henry Holt.

Daly, Lisa, and Miriam Beloglovsky. 2014. *Loose Parts: Inspiring Play in Young Children*. St. Paul, MN: Redleaf Press.

———. 2016. *Loose Parts 2: Inspiring Play with Infants and Toddlers*. St. Paul, MN: Redleaf Press.

———. 2018. *Loose Parts 3: Inspiring Culturally Sustainable Environments.* St. Paul, MN: Redleaf Press.

———. 2020. *Loose Parts 4: Inspiring 21st Century Learning.* St. Paul, MN: Redleaf Press.

Damon, Emma. 2005. *All Kinds of Homes.* London: Tango Books.

Denos, Julia. 2017. *Windows*. Somerville, MA: Candlewick Press.

DK. 2016. *Great City Maps: A Historical Journey through Maps, Plans, and Paintings*. London: DK.

Domus. 2016. "Mies van der Rohe: Architecture as Language." Domus, February 8. https://loves.domusweb.it/mies-van-der-rohe-architecture-as-language/.

Dougherty, Dale. 2012. "The Maker Movement." *Innovations*, MIT Press. Accessed July 25, 2019. www.mitpressjournals.org/doi/pdf/10.1162/INOV_a_00135.

Ellis, Carson. 2015. *Home*. Somerville, MA: Candlewick Press.

Felstiner, Sarah, Ann Pelo, and Margie Carter. 1999. *Thinking Big: Extending Emergent Curriculum Projects*. Hilltop Children's Center, Seattle. Harvest Resources (Film).

Finch, Mary. 2001. *The Three Billy Goats Gruff*. Cambridge, MA: Barefoot Books.

Fliess, Sue. 2016. *A Fairy Friend*. New York: Henry Holt.

Food Network. "Guide to Spices." Food Network. Accessed October 1, 2019. www.foodnetwork.com/recipes/articles/guide-to-spices.

Galdone, Paul. 1981. *The Three Billy Goats Gruff*. New York: Houghton Mifflin Harcourt.

Geisel, Theodore. 1971. *The Lorax*. New York. Random House.

Gibbons, Gail. 1990. *How a House Is Built*. New York: Holiday House.

Goldsworthy, Andy. 1990. *Andy Goldsworthy: A Collaboration with Nature*. New York: Abrams.

Guillian, Charlotte. 2017. *The Street beneath My Feet*. London: words & pictures.

Higgins, Chris. 2017. "How Many Combinations Are Possible Using 6 LEGO Bricks?" *Mental Floss*, February 12, 2017. http://mentalfloss.com/article/92127/how-many-combinations-are-possible-using-6-lego-bricks.

Hollingsworth, Patricia. 1993. "Making Connections through Architecture." *Gifted Child Today* 16 (5): 6–8.

Hutts Aston, Dianna. 2007. *A Seed Is Sleepy*. San Francisco: Chronicle.

George, Patrick. 2013. *Magic Colors.* New York: Boxer Books.

Gibbons, Gail. 1990. *How a House Is Built.* New York: Holiday House.

Hughes, Emily. 2018. *The Little Gardener*. London: Flying Eye Books.

Jeunesse, Gallimard. 1993. *Dinosaurs*. New York: Scholastic.

———. 1994. *The Rain Forest*. New York: Scholastic.

Jeunesse, Gallimard, Claude Delafosse, C. & D. Milett, and Nancy Krulik. 1993. *Castles.* New York: Scholastic.

Johnsen, Jan. 2017. *The Spirit of Stone*. Pittsburgh: St. Lynn's Press.

Johnson, Crockett. 1955. *Harold and the Purple Crayon*. New York: Harper & Brothers.

Jones, Rob. 2010. *See Inside Houses Long Ago.* London: Usborne.

Jung, Jin-Ho. 2018. *Look Up.* New York: Holiday House.

Juster, Norton. 1989. *The Phantom Tollbooth.* New York: Random House.

Kasprisin, Ray. 2016. *Play in Creative Problem-Solving for Planners and Architects.* New York: Routledge.

Knestrick, Jennifer. 2012. "The Zone of Proximal Development (ZPD) and Why It Matters for Early Childhood Learning." NWEA Education Blog. November 27. www.nwea.org/blog/2012/the-zone-of-proximal -development-zpd-and-why-it-matters-for-early-childhood-learning/.

Krause-Boelte, Maria, and Jon Kraus. 1881. *The Kindergarten Guide: An Illustrated Hand-Book*. Vol. 1, *The Gifts*. New York: E. Steiger.

Krauss, Ruth. (1952) 1989. *A Hole Is to Dig.* Reprint. New York: HarperCollins.

Lange, Alexandra. 2018. *The Design of Childhood: How the Material World Shapes Independent Kids*. New York: Bloomsbury.

Laroche, Giles. 2011. *If You Lived Here*. New York: Houghton Mifflin Harcourt.

Lionni, Leo. 1967. *Frederick*. New York: Pantheon.

Liu, C., S. L. Solis, H. Jensen, E. J. Hopkins, D. Neale, J. M. Zosh, K. Hirsh-Pasek, and D. Whitebread. 2017. *Neuroscience and Learning through Play: A Review of the Evidence* (research summary). The LEGO Foundation, DK.

Lockhart, Susanna. 2007. *If You See a Fairy Ring*. Hauppauge, NY: B.E.S. Publishing.

Louv, Richard. 2008. *Last Child in the Woods: Saving Our Children from Nature-Deficit Disorder.* Chapel Hill, NC: Algonquin Books.

Luera, Gail R., and Seong B. Hong. 2003. "A Collaborative Long-Term Project: Early Childhood Education, Environmental Education, and Landscape Architecture." *Canadian Children* 28 (1): 9–15.

Macken, JoAnn. 2008. *Digging Tunnels*. North Mankato, MN: Capstone.

Malaguzzi, Loris. 1993. "The Hundred Languages of Children." *The Hundred Languages of Children: The Reggio Emilia Approach to Early Childhood Education*, edited by Carolyn Edwards, Lella Gandini, and George Forman. Norwood, NJ: Ablex Publishing.

Mansfield, Andy. 2016. *Pop-Up New York*. New York: Lonely Planet Kids.

Maynor, Megan. 2018. *The Sandcastle That Lola Built*. New York: Knopf.

McCaulay, David. 1982. *Castle*. New York: Houghton Mifflin Harcourt.

McCloskey, Robert. 2016. *Make Way for Ducklings.* New York: Viking.

McLerran, Alice. *Roxaboxen*. New York: HarperCollins, 1991.

McRaven, Charles. 2007. *Stone Primer*. North Adams, MA: Storey Publishing.

Mettler, Rene. 2012. *The Egg.* New York: Scholastic.

Milne, A. A. 1988. *Winnie the Pooh.* New York: Dutton Books.

Mintzer, Mara. 2017. "How Kids Can Help Design Cities." TEDxMileHigh video, 14:25. www.ted.com/talks/mara_mintzer_how_kids_can_help_design _cities?language=en.

Mizielinska, Aleksandra, and Daniel Mizielinski. 2013. *Maps*. New York: Big Picture Press.

Moorhouse, Pete. 2018a. "Irresistible Learning: Woodwork in Early Childhood Education." Community Playthings. June 5. www.communityplaythings .com/resources/articles/2018/woodworking-with-kids.

———. 2018b. *Learning through Woodwork: Introducing Creative Woodwork in the Early Years*. New York: Routledge.

Morris, Ann. 1995. *Houses and Homes*. New York: HarperCollins.

Mulfinger, Dale. 2017. *The Family Cabin: Inspiration for Camps, Cottages, and Cabins*. Newtown, CT: Taunton Press.

Mullick, Nirvan. 2012. *Caine's Arcade.* April 9. http://cainesarcade.com.

Nicholson, Simon. 1971. "How NOT to Cheat Children: The Theory of Loose Parts." *Landscape Architecture* 62:30–34.

Noon, Steve. 1996. *Open House.* London: DK.

Olmon, Kyle. 2006. *Castle: Medieval Days and Knights*. New York: Orchard Books.

Portis, Antoinette. 2007. *Not a Stick*. New York: HarperCollins.

Potter, Giselle. 2016. *This Is My Dollhouse*. New York: Schwartz & Wade.

Radevsky, Anton. 2009. *The Architecture Pop-Up Book.* New York: Universe.

Ray, Jane. 2009. *The Dolls' House Fairy.* New York: Orchard Books.

Rosen, Michael. 2003. *We're Going on a Bear Hunt.* New York: Alladin.

Scarry, Richard. 1998. *Cars and Trucks and Things That Go*. New York: Little Golden Books.

———. 1999. *Best Word Book Ever.* New York: Little Golden Books.

———. 2015. *What Do People Do All Day?* New York: Little Golden Books.

Schaapman, Karina. 2014. *The Mouse Mansion*. New York: Dial Books.

Sheen, Dong Il, and Jae-Soo Liu. 2002. *Yellow Umbrella*. Ja Jolla, CA: Kane/ Miller.

Skeen, Patsy, and Anita Garner. 1984. *Woodworking for Young Children*. Washington, DC: NAEYC.

Stiles, David, and Jeanie Stiles. 2001. *Cabins: A Guide to Building Your Own Nature Retreat*. Ontario, Canada: Firefly Books.

Sterling, Debbie. 2013. TedX Talk.

Sweet, Roland. n.d. "Lincoln Logs: Everybody's First Log Cabin." Log Home Living. Accessed July 2, 2019: https://loghome.com/articles/article /lincoln-logs-everybodys-first-log-home.

Szymanski, Jennifer. 2019. *All about Bears*. Washington, DC: National Geographic Kids.

Tattersall, Ian. 2013. *In Search of the First Human Home.* Nautilus. December 5. http://nautil.us/issue/8/home/in-search-of-the-first-human-home.

Tekentrup, Britta. 2019. *Cat & Mouse*. New York: Prestel Publishing.

Turner, Christopher. 2011. *Toys of the Avant-Garde*. *ICON*, August 19. www.iconeye.com/design/features/item/9489-toys-of-the-avant-garde.

Wadell, Martin. 2002. *Owl Babies*. Somerville, MA: Candlewick Press.

Walsh, Liza Gardner. 2012. *Fairy House Handbook*. Camden, ME: Down East Books.

Willem, Mo. 2004. *Knuffle Bunny*. New York: Hyperion.

Van Dusen, Chris. 2012. *If I Built a House.* New York: Dial.

Wright, Hu-Van. 2014. *The Three Billy Goats Gruff.* Cambridge, MA: Starbright.